Eastern French Riviera

| 0 | 2 | 4 | 6 | 8 | 10 km |

| 0 | 2 | 4 | 6 miles |

INSIGHT GUIDES

NICE

& THE FRENCH RIVIERA
Step by Step

APA PUBLICATIONS

Part of the Langenscheidt Publishing Group

CONTENTS

ABOUT THIS BOOK

Above: the harbour at St-Tropez; pebble mosaic at the Bastion Musée Jean Cocteau, Menton; the Old Town of Vence; Musée Picasso, Antibes; looking out from boulevard de la Croisette at Cannes.

This *Step by Step Guide* has been produced by the editors of Insight Guides, whose books have set the standard for visual travel guides since 1970. With top-quality photography and authoritative recommendations, this guidebook brings you the very best of Nice and the French Riviera in a series of 14 tailor-made tours.

WALKS AND TOURS

The tours in the book provide something to suit all budgets, tastes and trip lengths. As well as covering the Riviera's many classic attractions and key towns and villages, the tours also take in lesser-known sights. The tours embrace a range of interests, so whether you are an art fan, a gourmet, a lover of flora or have kids to entertain, you will find an option to suit.

We recommend that you read the whole of a tour before setting out. This should help you to familiarise yourself with the route and enable you to plan where to stop for refreshments; options for this are shown in the 'Food and Drink' boxes, recog-nisable by the knife-and-fork sign, on most pages.

For our pick of the walks by theme, consult Recommended Tours For... *(see pp.6–7)*.

OVERVIEW

The tours are set in context by this introductory section, giving a regional overview to set the scene, plus background information on food and drink, shopping and entertainment. A succinct history timeline highlights the key events that have shaped Nice and the French Riviera over the centuries.

DIRECTORY

Also supporting the tours is a Directory chapter, comprising a user-friendly, clearly organised A–Z of practical information, our pick of where to stay while you are in the region and select restaurant listings; these eat-eries complement the more low-key cafés and restaurants that feature within the tours and are intended to offer a wider choice for evening din-ing. Also included here are some nightlife listings.

The Author

Paris-based journalist and editor Natasha Edwards is a regular contributor to Insight's French titles and also writes on travel and contemporary art and design for the *Daily Telegraph* and *Condé Nast Traveller* among other publications. Natasha has been visiting the French Riviera ever since moving to France in the 1990s. She finds it a region where the combination of cosmopolitan buzz and gor-geous colours and vegetation has an everlasting appeal and where there is still always something new to discover.

Margin Tips
Shopping tips, historical facts, handy hints and information on activities help visitors to make the most of their time in Nice and the French Riviera.

Feature Boxes
Notable topics are highlighted in these special boxes.

Key Facts Box
This box gives details of the distance covered on the tour, plus an estimate of how long it should take. It also states where the tour starts and finishes, and gives key travel information such as which days are best to do the tour or handy transport tips.

Route Map
Detailed cartography shows the tour clearly plotted with numbered dots. For more detailed mapping, see the pull-out map slotted inside the back cover.

Food and Drink
Recommendations of where to stop for refreshment are given in these boxes. The numbers prior to each restaurant/café name link to references in the main text. Restaurants in the Food and Drink boxes are plotted on the maps.

The € signs at the end of each entry reflect the approximate cost of a three-course dinner for one, or the most commonly taken set menu, not including wine. These should be seen as a guide only. Price ranges, also quoted on the inside back flap for easy reference, are:

€€€€	over 60 euros
€€€	40–60 euros
€€	25–40 euros
€	below 25 euros

Footers
Look here for the tour name, a map reference and the main attraction on the double-page spread.

GARDENERS

The Riviera's tropical vegetation is astonishing. Visit Val Rahmeh and the gardens of Menton (walk 8), Villa Ephrussi de Rothschild (tour 6), Domaine de Rayol in the Maures (tour 14) and Monaco's Jardin Exotique (walk 7).

RECOMMENDED TOURS FOR...

FOOD MARKETS

Succumb to the colourful fruit and vegetables at cours Saleya and the St-François fish market in Vieux Nice (walk 1), and the animated covered markets in Cannes (walk 11), Antibes (walk 10) and Menton (walk 8).

RETAIL THERAPY

Fashionistas can shop 'til they drop in Cannes (walk 11), Nice's Carré d'Or (walk 2) and the narrow streets of St-Tropez (walk 13), or try Nice's Vieux Port for antiques (walk 5).

SUPERB VIEWS

Get a bird's-eye view from the perched villages of Èze and Roquebrune (tour 6), look down on Vieux Nice from Colline du Château (walk 5) and gaze at the dazzling sea from the Corniche des Maures (tour 14).

PEOPLE-WATCHING

Enjoy celeb-spotting from a terrace on the Vieux Port in St-Tropez (walk 13), the obligatory stroll along La Croisette in Cannes (walk 11) and the comings and goings on place du Casino in Monte-Carlo (walk 7). Less chic but just as much fun is Nice's Promenade des Anglais (walk 2).

CHILDREN

Antibes (walk 10) and the Maures (tour 14) have lovely family-friendly sandy beaches, kids enjoy playing at knights in armour at the Citadelle in St-Tropez (walk 13), and the colourful fish are a winner at Monaco's Musée Océanographique (walk 7).

ARCHITECTURE AFICIONADOS

The region has a fascinating panoply of architecture: there's Baroque in Vieux Nice (walk 1) and Menton (walk 8); Belle Époque on Nice's promenade des Anglais (walk 2) or Cimiez district (walk 3), in Cannes (walk 11), Monte-Carlo (walk 7) and the Corniches (tour 6); and modern on Nice's Promenade des Arts (walk 4).

HISTORY BUFFS

Discover prehistoric humans near the Vieux Port in Nice (walk 5) or centuries of perfume making in Grasse (walk 12), or follow in the footsteps of Queen Victoria (walk 3) or Monégasque princes (walk 7).

YACHTING AND SAILING

Admire the craft in Europe's largest yachting marina at Antibes (walk 10) and the luxury charters at St-Tropez (walk 13), Cannes (walk 11) and Monaco (walk 7). Learn to sail at Bormes-les-Mimosas (tour 14) and Nice's Vieux Port (walk 5).

MODERN ART LOVERS

The south of France was a hub of the 20th-century avant-garde. Visit Matisse and Chagall museums in Cimiez (walk 3), the castle where Picasso had his studio in Antibes (walk 10) and Matisse's chapel in Vence (walk 9). Discover the École de Nice at Mamac (walk 4).

OVERVIEW

An overview of Nice and the French Riviera's geography,
customs and culture, plus illuminating background information
on food and drink, shopping, entertainment, festivals and history.

INTRODUCTION

From the Belle Époque sweep of Nice's promenade des Anglais to Romanesque cathedrals and medieval hill villages, the French Riviera offers an intriguing mix of the grandiose and the intimate along with a variety of architecture just waiting to be discovered.

It is the colours you notice first: stucco houses of all tones from cream via amber to deep russet; the white limestone crags of the Alpes-Maritimes against the blue of the Mediterranean Sea; and the red sandstones, grey schists, green serpentine and cork oaks of the Var. Together with the Riviera's luscious vegetation, vibrant flowers, green-grey olive trees and diverse vegetables overflowing from market stalls, these elements create a brilliant palette of hues – offset by the southern sun – which has inspired Signac, Dufy, Matisse and countless other artists over the years.

GEOGRAPHY AND LAYOUT

The walks and tours in this guide first explore Nice (capital of the Alpes-Maritimes *département*), then they focus on the coastal strip between Menton by the Italian frontier to the east and Cannes in the west, before heading inland to Grasse and Vence in the Pre-Alp foothills, and westwards as far as St-Tropez and the rugged Massif des Maures in the neighbouring region of Var.

Town Layouts

The Riviera's history and climate have largely determined the layout of its towns. Most are characterised by an Old Town in the centre, where a tight maze of medieval streets and stairways often grew up around a church or defensive keep, and tall houses and narrow streets ensured shade and relative cool even in summer.

From the 19th century, New Towns developed around them; these were characterised by neoclassical, Belle Époque and Art Deco terraces and villas, whether laid out on a grid as in Nice's New Town or romantically meandering as in Nice's Cimiez district and Cannes' Croix des Gardes.

Beyond often lies a sprawl of modern public housing estates and suburban apartment blocks and houses. The demands of both permanent residents and mass tourism have sometimes led to seemingly uncontrolled construction, where, beyond a few exclusive peninsulas, the dense *betonisation* (concreting-up) of the coast has in places turned the Riviera from an idyllic destination into an urban nightmare of strip development.

Hivernales
While the French Riviera is now chiefly a summer destination, Nice is a great city to visit all year round. In winter or springtime, museums are less crowded, the arts season is in full swing, hotels and restaurants remain open and sunshine is still almost always guaranteed.

CLIMATE

A Mediterranean climate of hot dry summers, mild winters and sun that shines for more than 300 days a year has always been one of the area's attractions, although dramatic thunderstorms in late summer and in autumn, when torrential rain occasionally causes flash flooding, are not unknown. Global warming and overdevelopment have contributed to fears of rivers drying up, shortages of water and the risk of summer fires.

HISTORY AND ARCHITECTURE

Prehistoric cave dwellers, Phocaean traders, Roman garrisons and medieval monks and warlords have all left traces. However, the French Riviera's architectural heritage was largely shaped by power struggles between French-ruled Provence and the Italian-dominated Comté de Nice – which has given such an Italianate flavour to Vieux Nice – as well as battles for control of the Mediterranean between France, Spain and Italy.

The 16th and 17th centuries saw the construction of citadels at Villefranche-sur-Mer and St-Tropez and the star-shaped fortifications of Antibes. The Wars of Religion and Counter-Reformation backlash have left the area peppered with ornate Baroque churches and chapels full of starbursts, loud marble and cherubs

intended to reinforce the Catholic faith. Outside Vieux Nice, the city reflects first the planning ambitions of the kings of Sardinia-Piedmont, with the elegant, classical, arcaded place Masséna and place Garibaldi, and after 1860, of its new Second-Empire French rulers, with its grid of streets, train station and the busy thoroughfare, avenue Jean Médecin.

But the area's history has also been moulded by its visitors, leaving a legacy of cheerfully eclectic Belle Époque seaside architecture evident in flouncy palatial hotels, extravagant villas, neo-Gothic Anglican churches and exotic domed Russian Orthodox churches, as well as remarkable gardens, created by the green-fingered who introduced an extraordinary array of tropical plants.

Modern Innovation

If a lot of recent seaside apartment blocks are remarkably banal, clearly caring more about balconies with sea views than aesthetics or innovation, there is also some exciting modern architecture to discover, such as the Musée Chagall and along the promenade des Arts in Nice, and Menton's new Cocteau museum designed by Rudy Ricciotti, due to open in 2011.

Pétanque

Whether it is on the beach in Nice, by the river in rural Collobrières (where it now features on the primary school curriculum), under the plane trees on place des Lices in St-Tropez or the gravelly allées de la Liberté in Cannes, an enduring love of *pétanque* should dispel any doubts that you are truly in the south of France. Indeed any patch of vaguely flat land would appear ample excuse for men – it is still a largely male pastime – to get together for a game.

Derived from ancient *boules* and the *jeu provençal*, *pétanque* acquired its name *péts* or *pieds tanqués*, meaning 'feet together' (as there is no run-up and players throw the ball from within a small circle), in 1910. The use of steel rather than nailed wooden balls became established in the 1920s.

One of the game's pleasures is that anyone can have a go – the Café in St-Tropez even lends balls to its customers – but tactics, throwing skills and mastering exactly the right expressions of doubt, confidence, bemusement and disbelief can take years of practice.

POPULATION

With a population of 350,000, Nice is France's fifth city, and lies at the heart of a conurbation of nearly 900,000 of the *département*'s 1,056,000 inhabitants. These figures reveal a vast difference between the densely populated coastal strip and sparsely inhabited interior.

Young and Cosmopolitan

Despite its dowager reputation, Nice is actually a surprisingly young city. Fifty percent of its population is aged under 40, with a growing student population. Some 26,000 students are enrolled at the Université Nice Sophia Antipolis, which has a growing reputation, notably for law, social sciences and scientific research. There are also huge seasonal variations in numbers. A resort like St-Tropez swells to over 35,000 in the summer and settles back to a villagey 5,500 in winter.

The poplulation is also distinguished by its high proportion of incomers, reflecting not just France's traditional immigration from North and West Africa, Southeast Asia, Portugal, Spain and Italy, or expat communities of Britons, Russians and Germans, but also by that from other regions of France. Today, curiously, the Riviera's foreign population is not unlike its composition at the end of the 19th century, with the return of Russians and eastern Europeans and the numerous

British who have brought property in Vieux Nice, Antibes or the Grasse hinterland, although its social make-up is not necessarily the same; young Britons are often here to work and the Russians represent not old aristocracy but new fortunes.

LOCAL CUSTOMS

The influx of all these immigrants and émigrés from both France and abroad has led some to say that there has been a dilution of local culture. True, the south is capable of doing Provençal stereotypes to excess: the garish print tablecloths and dirndl skirts you will find in souvenir shops and markets have little to do with the subtlety of the original wood-block *indienne* prints, and rows of chirping pottery cicadas and olive-sprigged jugs are far from the functional spirit of true Provençal pottery. Yet the area's inhabitants remain firmly attached to local traditions: a game of *pétanque (see feature)*; the herbs, anchovies and olives of the region's distinctive cuisine and snacks; and festivities, some of which go back for centuries. St-Tropez has celebrated patron saint Torpes with the Bravades in May for over 500 years, even snooty Monaco continues to burn its boat for Saint Devota, and visit Nice or Menton at carnival time and you will find hundreds of locals participating in lively festivals that are not just put on for tourists.

ECONOMY AND POLITICS

However, tourism is a major component of the southern economy, with Nice boasting the highest number of hotel beds after Paris and more than 4 million visitors a year. Cannes is also a year-round luxury tourist destination. The region's other industries include agriculture, wine and food processing, perfumes at Grasse, property development, advertising and science. Financial and banking services are important in Monaco, which smarts at being on the tax haven blacklist but continues to maintain a reputation for secrecy.

Although Nice faces many of the problems of a big modern city, such as the integration of its immigrant population and high unemployment, it is also a flourishing administrative centre and the leading congress town after Paris, thanks to France's second-largest airport; the city's 10,000 hotel rooms and the facilities offered by its Acropolis congress centre; and the emerging Arénas district near the airport.

Looking to the Future

Meanwhile, under dynamic new mayor Christian Estrosi, Nice continues to look ahead, with plans for a second tram line and the development of the Plaine du Var as an ecological zone, comprising a business district, football stadium and expanded port facilities, built according to the principles of sustainable development.

Above from far left: Nice is a fantastic destination for enjoying art and sculpture, such as at the Musée d'Art Moderne et Contemporain; open-air fruit and vegetable markets abound.

Langues d'Oc
Although the official language is French, you may still hear snatches of Nissart and Provençal dialect, descended from Occitane, the ancient Low Latin language of the troubadours. Street signs in the Old Towns are often bilingual: look for the Nissart *carrièra* or Provençal *carriero* meaning *rue* or street, and *castelét* or *castelar* for *château* or castle.

FOOD AND DRINK

The French Riviera's diverse fruit and vegetable produce combined with olive oil and aromatic herbs typify local dishes. However, Provençal cuisine comes in a variety of styles, from hearty, age-old peasant stews to simple lightly grilled fish, and is another of the region's best attributes.

Eating out is one of the great pleasures of travelling in France, and the French Riviera has restaurants for all moods, occasions and budgets. A grand gastronomic restaurant with its white table linen, silver cloches and plethora of waiters serving elaborate preparations is very different prospect to a tiny hole-in-the-wall bistro with just one or two cooks and servers, yet each in its own way may be just as good. And at beach restaurants, which might literally have tables on the sand, the emphasis may be as much on DJs and sea views as on cuisine.

LOCAL SPECIALITIES

Olives and Olive Oil

Olive oil rather than butter is used for cooking and is a crucial ingredient in *anchoïade* (also known as *bagna cauda*), a warm anchovy and olive oil sauce, into which chopped raw vegetables are dipped, and *aïoli* (garlic mayonnaise), which may appear as an appetiser dip or as the ceremonial *grand aïoli* – traditionally a Friday or Christmas Eve dish – where it is served with assorted raw vegetables, cod, whelks, boiled potatoes and eggs. Black or green olives are at the base of *tapenade*, a purée of olives and capers delicious spread on toast or as an accompaniment to fish. Nice's tiny purplish-black *cailletier* olive turns up in many dishes; *à la niçoise* will often indicate a sauce made with tomatoes, onions and black olives, and may be found accompanying pasta, fish, chicken or rabbit.

Vegetable Cornucopia

Superb tomatoes, courgettes of different hues and purple aubergines give Riviera cuisine its palette of colours. Preparations can be as simple as marinated red peppers – a favourite starter – or the fresh herbs and mixed young salad leaves of *mesclun*. Tomatoes appear as simple salads, chilled summer soups or as *tomates provençales*, accompanying meat and fish dishes, sprinkled with minced garlic and breadcrumbs and baked very slowly until almost caramelised. Nice's most celebrated vegetable dish is *ratatouille*, a luscious combination of tomatoes, onions, garlic, courgettes, peppers and aubergines. Look out also for *caponata*, aubergine stewed with tomatoes and capers.

You will also find all manner of vegetable *tians*, baked gratins perhaps of courgette, squash or aubergine with egg and rice, named after the *tian* (rectangular earthenware dish) in which they are cooked. Tiny purple artichokes, almost without a choke, are braised *à la barigoule* with mushrooms and bacon, but can also be sliced very finely and eaten raw. Another treat is delicate orange-yellow courgette flowers, dipped in egg and flour and deep fried as fritters. *Blettes* (Swiss chard) is served as a vegetable or combined with apples, raisins and pine kernels in Nice's *tourte de blettes*, a surprisingly sweet tart, while stuffed cabbage, the leaves bound around a sausage meat filling, is a rustic speciality of Cannes and Grasse.

Fish

Not surprisingly given the French Riviera's glorious coastline and the trend for healthy eating, fish features heavily on the menu, especially at beach restaurants and the restaurants that line the ports in Villefranche-sur-Mer, Nice, St-Jean-Cap-Ferret and St-Tropez. However, overfishing of the Mediterranean and the decline of the Riviera's fishing fleet mean that apart from the grandest restaurants, which still buy directly from the remaining artisanal fishermen, much of the fish now comes from France's Breton and Atlantic ports. Common species include *loup* or *daurade* (sea bream), *rouget* (red mullet), *saint-pierre* (John Dory) and *thon* (tuna), as well as *seiche* or *calamar* (squid) and *poulpe* (octopus).

Sardines are a speciality in Nice, stuffed with Swiss chard, marinaded or grilled; likewise, *estocaficada* (*stockfisch* in Cannes, *stocafi* in Monaco) or salt cod, which is stewed in wine, tomatoes and olives. You will find the fish stew bouillabaisse (originally from Marseille) all along the coast, served in two courses, first the saffron-coloured soup accompanied by garlicky *rouille*, and then the fish and boiled potatoes. *Moules* (mussels), cultivated in the bay of Toulon, are very popular in the Var resorts of Bormes-les-Mimosas, Cavalaire and Le Lavandou.

Above from far left: olives, chillies and garlic at the food market on cours Saleya in Nice.

Below: fresh fish at the Marché Forville in Cannes.

On Course

The classic French meal consists of an *entrée* (starter), *plat* (main course) and dessert, and perhaps cheese course before dessert (and both fish and meat courses in grand restaurants). However, it is also perfectly acceptable, especially at lunch-time, to just order an *entrée* and *plat* or *plat* and dessert.

Meat

Meat is not forgotten, however. This is France: almost every brasserie will have a *steak frites* on its menu, or go for succulent *daube de boeuf*, beef stewed in red wine and herbs with a touch of orange zest. Rabbit is also common, roasted with herbs or cooked *à la niçoise* with white wine, olives and tomatoes. The best lamb comes from the Alpine hinterland, while in winter you will find plenty of game in the Maures and Niçois back country.

Cheeses and Desserts

The Côte d'Azur is not a major dairying or cheese-making area, but you will find some mountain-style Tomme cow's milk cheeses from the Mercantour as well as farm-produced goat's cheese *(chèvre)* from the Maures and Alpine foothills. These range from young, moist, fresh cheeses to harder, drier *crottins*. Among specialities are *poivre d'âne*, goat's cheese rolled in summer savory; tiny goat's cheeses marinaded in olive oil and herbs; and *brousse*, a ricotta-like fresh cheese used in dips and desserts.

Desserts are mostly based around fruit, including figs baked in tarts, gratins and crumbles, and lemon meringue tart *(tarte au citron meringué)* made with the little lemons of Menton. Fashionable desserts include summer fruit soups and creations inspired by nostalgia for children's caramel bars and strawberry sweets.

Cuisine Niçoise

Nice's distinctive cuisine is a unique fusion of Provençal and Italianate influences that come from the town's Savoyard past and its market gardening tradition. *Ratatouille* and *salade niçoise* (salad with tuna, olives, peppers, broad beans, eggs and anchovies) have travelled the world, others remain essentially local. The *pan bagnat* is like a portable snack version of *salade niçoise* in a roll. *Pissaladière* is a sort of thin, open, onion tart, garnished with anchovies and olives; the Menton variant *tarte mentonnaise* also includes tomatoes. Nice claims to have invented ravioli, but here, unlike those found in Italy, they are typically filled with left-over *daube de boeuf (see above)* and Swiss

Bellet Wines

Head north out of Nice towards St-Roman-de-Bellet (or take the no. 11 or 62 bus) and you come across one of France's smallest wine appellations; the only one technically cultivated entirely within a city boundary. In a tradition going back over two thousand years to the Phocaean Greeks of Nikaia, vines are planted on the precipitous narrow terraces of the Alpine foothills, with just 50ha (124 acres) of vines and just over a dozen producers, among them Château de Bellet and Domaine de la Source. High altitude and lots of wind and sunshine produce dry, fruity whites, light rosés and long-keeping spicy reds; however, Bellet's recent return to fashion and tiny scale of production means that the wines can be rather expensive. Most vineyards will receive visitors by appointment (see www.vinsdebellet.com).

chard. Other Italianate specialities include gnocchi, made from potatoes or durum wheat, and *soupe au pistou*, a minestrone-like vegetable and bean soup into which a dollop of basil *pistou* (pesto) is stirred at the end.

Perhaps the most characteristic of all Niçois dishes is *petits farcis*, an assortment of stuffed tomatoes, aubergines, courgettes, onions and bell peppers, each with its own slightly different filling, based around variants of cooked ham, rice, herbs, minced meat and breadcrumbs, and served warm or cold.

WHERE TO EAT

As well as the elegant dining rooms of Belle Époque *grands hotels*, family-run eateries and über-cool celebrity-chef dining destinations, there are also many Italian restaurants, especially in Monaco and Menton with their large Italian populations. A recent dining trend is the rise of wine bistros where good market-inspired dishes are accompanied by a wide choice of wines by the glass.

Café-brasseries typically mutate over the course of a day, from casual breakfast spot to full-scale restaurant at lunchtime, afternoon coffee haunt, early evening drinks rendezvous and back to restaurant in the evening. Some serve simple steaks and salads all day long, convenient when you are exploring a city and are not always in the right place at meal times. Those on the promenade des Anglais often seem best suited for

breakfast, those on the port at St-Tropez are unmissable for observing yachts and passers-by at aperitif hour.

In Vieux Nice and Le Suquet in Cannes, many restaurants seem to have changed little for generations, still serving up age-old local specialities. Elsewhere, adventurous chefs, often haute-cuisine trained, are injecting new influences and creations. At such places, you might find on one hand modern experimental preparations, such as colourful purées and foamy emulsions, and fashionable presentations in glass jars; on the other hand, a return to roots – sometimes literally (think beetroot, radishes, parsnips, jerusalem artichokes and purple carrots) – and slow cooking in cast-iron casseroles.

WHAT TO DRINK

Most wine lists have a good choice of Provençal wines, including Côtes de Provence (which comes in all three colours), vast amounts of light, summery rosé, more substantial Bandol wines, and the southern Rhône appellations, such as Châteauneuf-du-Pape, Coteaux d'Aix-en-Provence and Côtes du Luberon. Something you will probably only ever see on a wine list in Nice are the rare yet fashionable Bellet wines *(see feature, left)*.

The quintessential southern aperitif is pastis, made from anise and assorted plants and herbs, always diluted with water to turn a cloudy pale yellow.

Above from far left: ice cream stall on cours Saleya; al fresco evening dining.

Below: wine from the Côtes du Rhône; Absinthe Bar in Antibes *(see p.77)*.

SHOPPING

As much as for sightseeing, the French Riviera is a great shopping destination, whether you are after designer fashion, the right look for the beach or regional arts and crafts.

Small individual shops and markets remain an essential part of the French lifestyle, although very touristy locations, such as St-Paul-de-Vence, have been taken over almost entirely by souvenir shops and arts-and-crafts galleries. Chic boutiques selling ultra-smart clothes and accessories at ultra-expensive prices abound in all the fashionable coastal resorts and large towns, while all along the coast you will find plenty of crafts workshops displaying a tempting array of top-quality original gifts with affordable price tags (for the most part).

Les Soldes
Sale dates in January and late June to July are set by the Ministry of Finance. They usually begin on a Wednesday and last five weeks, but may vary slightly according to the *département*, allowing tourist areas to start their sales during the holiday period. Individual shops are also allowed two weeks of special 'promotions' over the rest of the year.

FASHION

As France's fifth city, Nice offers everything from classic French designer fashion to cheap-and-cheerful teen styles. There are several distinct shopping districts. Smart clothes and designer labels are concentrated in the New Town along avenue de Suède, avenue de Verdun and rue Paradis, and hot young designers on rue Alphonse Karr. Rue de France and rue Masséna contain more mainstream chainstores, as does avenue Jean Médecin, home to the Centre Étoile shopping centre and

practical supermarket Monoprix. Vieux Nice tends towards new-agey clothes, craft jewellery and souvenirs.

In Cannes, for diamond necklaces and *haute-couture* evening dresses suitable for walking up the steps during the Film Festival, try the prestigious boutiques clustered on boulevard de la Croisette. Younger styles, such as Zadig & Voltaire and Italian labels Missoni and Patrizia Pepe, can be found beside more mass-market chains and plenty of glitz on rue d'Antibes. Rue Meynadier, near the Marché Forville, is lined with cheaper outlets for casual wear and beachgear.

Monaco also abounds in designer labels, albeit of a more conservative bent than those in Cannes. Monaco's 'golden rectangle' is around the place du Casino, rue des Beaux Arts and the upmarket Galerie du Métropole; more boutiques can be found on avenue Princesse Grace and boulevard des Moulins.

Reflecting its starlet-and-villager dichotomy, St-Tropez's outlets range from designer labels like Dior to home-grown Atelier Rondini's Tropézienne gladiator-style sandals made since 1927 to casual yachting wear.

There are plenty of good clothes shops in Vieux Antibes, although here the style is more understated chic; think the nautical style of Bleu Blanc and handcrafted jewellery.

For the Beach

Swimwear and beachgear can be a good buy all along the coast, especially at summer sale time. Most resorts have a wide range of swimsuits, sunhats and flipflops. For men and boys, true chic is St-Tropez's Villebrequin brand, with three boutiques in St-Tropez and outlets in Nice, Cannes and Monaco.

ARTS AND CRAFTS

Souvenirs run the gamut from clichéd pottery cicadas, herb mills with olive sprig motifs, and colourful Provençal print fabrics, to genuine craft pottery such as *tians* (baking dishes) and authentic basketware. Many towns, like Antibes, Bormes-les-Mimosas and Villefranche-sur-Mer, have summer craft markets that typically sell soaps, bags, pottery and jewellery. Èze has plenty of tourist tack, but you will also find attractive olive-wood bowls and chopping boards just inside the Posterne gate, and high-quality art galleries and potteries in Vieux Vence, notably on rue de l'Evêché and rue Henri Isnard. Near Antibes, Vallauris is home to countless art potteries, while Biot is known for its handblown bubble glass.

Perfumes can be a good buy in Grasse, where boutiques such as Fragonard sell their own scents and beauty products at factory prices. Look out also for the artisanal soaps and bath products made by the Savonnerie de Bormes in Bormes-les-Mimosas.

FOOD AND WINE

The Riviera abounds in tempting food shops and markets that are ideal for sampling local produce, stocking up for picnics and observing local life. Good items to take home include olive oil, table olives, olive paste and *tapenade*. The Nice area has an *appellation d'origine contrôlée* (AOC) for oil made from its *cailletier* olive. Reputable outlets include Alviari on rue St-François-de-Paule, which presses oil at its own mill, and Oliviera on rue du Collet, both in Vieux Nice, and the 1760-built Moulin du Rossignol in Grasse. You can usually taste before buying.

For sweet treats, go for chocolates, candied fruit and other gourmet items from Maison Auer in Vieux-Nice, candied fruits and violet- and rose-flavoured lollipops, chocolates and jams from Confiserie Florian by Nice's Vieux Port, and at Pont du Loup between Vence and Grasse. Marrons glacés from Collobrières in the Massif des Maures are another local speciality.

Other regional produce includes Côtes de Provence wines produced on the Cap Brégançon and St-Tropez peninsula, Bellet wines *(see p.16)*, pastis and local aperitifs such as *vin d'oranger* and *pêche de vigne*.

ENTERTAINMENT

The French Riviera's nightclubs and casinos are all part of the south of France's hedonist image, but there are plenty of cultural attractions to suit more highbrow tastes as well.

Between them, Nice, Cannes, St-Tropez and Monte-Carlo offer a comprehensive all-year cultural programme, which ranges from early music to modern theatre, casinos, nightclubs and international pop. For contact details of venues, see the relevant Walks and Tours chapters and the Nightlife chapter *(pp.122–3)*.

THEATRE

The leading venue for interesting modern theatre is the Théâtre National de Nice, which is dedicated to presenting contemporary drama and known for the number of new plays it premieres. Founded in 1969 as part of a state-subsidised policy of regionalisation, the theatre moved into its premises on the promenade des Arts in 1989 *(see p.123)*. Other venues in Nice include the Théâtre de la Cité, as well as offbeat fringe productions at Le Bar des Oiseaux. Also worth checking out are the small yet dynamic Antibea Théâtre in Antibes and Grasse's striking modern Théâtre de Grasse, which puts on a multidisciplinary mix of theatre, dance, music and circus by visiting companies.

DANCE

The most prestigious dance company is the Ballets de Monte-Carlo, descendant of Diaghilev's Ballets Russes. The company has regained its avant-garde reputation under choreographer Jean-Christophe Maillot, and now performs in the Grimaldi Forum (www.grimaldi forum.com) or the Casino terrace when not touring internationally. For works by visiting French and international choreographers, the biennial Cannes dance festival (www.festivaldedanse-cannes.com) is a must, while hip-hop, flamenco and contemporary dance also feature at Nice's Théâtre Lino Ventura.

ROCK AND POP

Big names of French pop and international rock perform at the Acropolis and Palais Nikaia in Nice, the Palais des Festivals in Cannes, and the Sporting d'Eté and Sporting d'Hiver in Monaco, with a smaller, more intimate setting for rock, jazz and blues at Moods in Monte-Carlo (www.montecarloresort.com). Nice's Théâtre Lino Ventura focuses more on recent urban and electronic music trends. There's also an active pub

What's On?
To find out what's going on, look out for free brochures, such as Nice's *Saison des Cultures* and *Rendez-Vous à Nice*, *Sortir à Cannes* and *Le Mois à Menton*, available in hotels and tourist offices. Other good sources are *La Semaine des Spectacles* and the cultural pages of daily newspaper *Nice Matin* available from newsstands.

rock scene, mainly catering to the large Anglophone expat crowd, with bands playing venues like Ma Nolan's pub in Nice *(see p.51)*, Monaco's La Rascasse *(see p.61)* and the bars of Vieux Antibes.

CLASSICAL MUSIC AND OPERA

Opulent red velvet, gilding and chandeliers are all part of the experience at the Opéra de Nice and Salle Garnier opera house in Monaco. Big gala-style opera productions are staged at Nice's Palais Nikaia, the Opéra de Nice (home of the Orchestre Philharmonique) and Monaco's Grimaldi Forum. Look out for the Ensemble Baroque de Nice (www.ensemblebaroquedenice.org), which performs in the Baroque churches and chapels of Vieux Nice and nearby towns. It aims to give authentic interpretations of 17th- and 18th-century music performed on early instruments and has a reputation for rediscovering forgotten pieces. Experimental contemporary music is the focus of the Cirm institute, which organises the Manca festival (www.cirm-manca.org) in November.

CINEMA

The Riviera itself stars in numerous films, whether it is *James Bond* at the Casino de Monte-Carlo, car chases along the Corniches or the French comedy *Brice de Nice*. With France home to the largest film industry in Europe, cinema-going is a major activity here, with an appetite for everything from homegrown films and Hollywood blockbusters to Middle Eastern cinema.

For non-French films, check whether they are screened in VO *(version originale* – original language with French subtitles) or VF *(version française)* dubbed into French. All year round the Cinémathèque de Nice puts on themed seasons and retrospectives. Open-air cinemas are popular in summer, such as those at Villefranche-sur-Mer and Monaco, with a different film each night in VO on a giant screen.

NIGHTLIFE

During Cannes' Film Festival, many Parisian clubs migrate south for special parties; in summer, party-goers head for Juan-les-Pins and St-Tropez, where in addition to hard-to-get-into clubs, there are also more relaxed lounge bars and a party scene on the resort's private beaches. Nice's nightlife is more centred on lounge bars and there is also a gay club scene, led by long-standing Le Klub. The Riviera is also famed for its casinos. Leading the glamour stakes are the Casino de Monte-Carlo and Croisette casinos in Cannes, while more staid casinos, dominated by slot machines, are found in Beaulieu and Menton. Spanning the discothèque-casino spectrum are La Siesta, on the beach east of Antibes, and Cannes' Palm Beach.

Above from far left: fast cars and glamour at the Casino de Monte-Carlo; Ballets de Monte-Carlo; the Théâtre National de Nice stages contemporary works.

FESTIVALS

More than anywhere else in the country, the French Riviera is a whirl-wind of arts festivals over the summer season. Away from the action, even small villages have their own celebrations throughout the year.

When the main arts venues close in high summer, their place is taken by cultural events ranging from classical music and jazz festivals to electronic music parties, most of them outdoors, and popular films screened on the beach. All year, there's a roster of celebrations for everything from flowers to obscure saints, often with origins dating back centuries.

MUSIC AND THE PERFORMING ARTS

Classical, Opera and Dance

One of the oldest cultural events on the coast is Menton's chamber music festival (www.festivalmusiquementon. com; Aug). Along with big-name ensembles and singers, there are inexpensive 6pm concerts where you can pick out the talents of the future.

Opera is the focus of Musiques aux Coeur (www.antibesjuanlespins.com; early July), held in the lovely gardens of Villa Eilenroc on Cap d'Antibes and Les Azuriales (www.lesazuriales. com; late Aug) at the Villa Ephrussi de Rothschild on St-Jean-Cap-Ferrat.

In Cannes there are classical concerts in Les Nuits Musicales du Suquet

(www.nuitsdusuquet-cannes.com; July), while in Monaco the acclaimed Ballets de Monte-Carlo perform in Les Nuits de la Danse (July) on the terrace of the Casino.

World, Rock and Pop

Despite Menton's retirement home image, it has recently rejuvenated its arts scene with the Festival Créole (www. menton.fr; July), featuring dance, music and food from France's Caribbean and Indian Ocean *départements*, and Ma Ville est Tango (www.tango-menton. com; July). In Vence, Les Nuits du Sud (www.nuitsdusud.com; mid-July–mid-Aug) sees some of the best names in world music performing in the place du Grand Jardin, with plenty of free concerts too. Meanwhile, Monte-Carlo Sporting Summer Festival (www.sport ingmontecarlo.com; July and Aug) rolls out big international rock names and golden-oldie comebacks (Seal, Lily Allen, Moby, Johnny Hallyday and Leonard Cohen in 2009) at the Sporting d'Eté on Avenue Princesse Grace.

Jazz and Electronica

Nice and Juan-les-Pins vie for the title of southern jazz capital. Jazz à Juan (www.jazzajuan.com; mid-July) held in the Pinède Gould, was founded in tribute to saxophonist Sidney Bechet, who composed *Petit Fleur* and *Dans les rues d'Antibes* when living in Antibes; while Nice Jazz Festival *(see p.41)* also includes rock and blues. Festival Pantiero (www.festivalpantiero.com; Aug) on the terrace of the Palais des Festivals has quickly established itself as the place for the latest electronic music trends.

Theatre and Stand-Up

On the hill above St-Tropez, Ramatuelle's theatre festival (www.festival deramatuelle.com; July–Aug) puts the emphasis on one-person shows and classic comedy theatre, performed by well-known actors in a spectacular 1200-seat amphitheatre. For a more alternative scene, try the Festival du Rire (www.festival-rire.com; Sept), a week of café-théâtre and stand-up comedy at St-Raphael.

Off-Season Festivals

A few big arts festivals take place over the rest of the year. As well as the celebrated Film Festival each May, Cannes' dance biennial (www.festivaldedanse-cannes.com; Nov and Dec, next in 2011) features top dance companies from across Europe, while the Festival International du Cirque de Monte-Carlo (www.montecarlofestivals.com; Jan), held under the big top in Fontvieille, is renowned as a springboard for breathtaking new circus talents.

FOLKLORE AND FIREWORKS

In St-Tropez, Roman centurion Torpes is celebrated in the Bravades de St-Tropez on 16 and 17 May, while in Monaco Corsican saint Devota is remembered with a ceremonial boat burning on the eve of her fête on 26 January. The carnival tradition remains strong in the weeks leading up to Lent: the biggest event is Nice Carnaval (www.nicecarnaval.com; Feb) when spectacular giant floats parade along the promenade des Anglais, while in Villefranche-sur-Mer traditional carnival kings are replaced by a watery *bataille des fleurs* from boats in the port.

Menton's Fête du Citron has bands and floats along the seafront and spectacular sculptures made of oranges and lemons in the Jardin Biovès (www.fete ducitron.com; Feb), and in late February, extravagant floats decorated with mimosa and other flowers parade around Bormes-les-Mimosas (www.bormeslesmimosas.com). In August, perfume town Grasse marks the start of the jasmine harvest with floral floats and brass bands in the Fête du Jasmin (www.ville-grasse.fr).

There are spectacular summer fireworks displays in Cannes and Monaco, while St-Raphael's Fêtes de la Lumière (www.saint-raphael.com) celebrates Christmas with fireworks, floodlighting, street theatre and Father Christmas who arrives by boat.

Above from far left:
Menton's Fête du Citron is renowned for its colourful displays; Menton's chamber music festival is in August.

HISTORY: KEY DATES

Long and turbulent, the history of the Riviera saw waves of successive rulers, and traces of their presence remain today. More recently, the area's beauty, light and climate attracted artists and foreign nobility, as well as mass tourism.

FROM PREHISTORY TO THE ROMANS

400,000 BC	Prehistoric elephant hunters camp out at Terra Amata.
5thC BC	Phocaean Greeks from Marseille set up trading posts at Nikaia (Nice), Antipolis (Antibes) and Monoikos (Monaco).
2ndC BC	The Romans colonise southern France.
1stC AD	Cemenelum (Cimiez, Nice) becomes the capital of Roman province of Alpes Maritimae.

DARK AND MIDDLE AGES

5th–7thC	The barbarian invasions; Saracens establish strongholds at Èze, Ramatuelle and La Garde Freinet, but are expelled by 972.
1144	Nice becomes quasi-independent, ruled by elected consuls.
1246	Charles d'Anjou marries Béatrice de Provence and becomes Count of Provence, ruling over Anjou, Provence, Naples and Sicily.
1295	François Grimaldi, disguised as a monk, takes control of Monaco.
1388	Nice forms alliance with dukes of Savoy and declares separation from Provence under the Dédition of Nice.
1481	Cannes, Vence and the area west of the River Var (but not Nice or Monaco) become part of France. Thereafter, the region sees conflicts between Savoy-controlled Nice and French-controlled Provence.

RENAISSANCE AND BAROQUE ERAS

1538	The Treaty of Nice is negotiated by Pope Paul III between François 1er and Emperor Charles V.
1543	The siege of Nice by French and Turkish armies.
16thC	The Wars of Religion begin: the reformist bishop is thrown out of Vence; the Counter-Reformation Baroque style dominates in Nice.
1680–98	Antibes is fortified by Louis XIV's military architect Vauban.

| 1706 | Louis XIV razes Nice's citadel. |
| 1731 | English visitors winter for the first time in Nice. |

Above from far left: King François 1er and Emperor Charles V discuss the Treaty of Nice; poster advertising the winter season in 1920s Nice.

REVOLUTION AND EMPIRE

| 1789 | French Revolution: three years later, Revolutionary troops take Nice. |
| 1815 | Napoleon escapes from Elba and spends night in Cannes before marching on Paris via Grasse and the Alps for the 'Hundred Days' in power. |

BIRTH OF TOURISM

1822	The construction of the Promenade des Anglais.
1834	Lord Henry Brougham discovers Cannes.
1860	Nice joins France after a referendum; Monaco relinquishes its rights to Menton and Roquebrune, which had also voted to join France.
1863	Monte-Carlo's casino opens.
1864	The railway reaches Nice from Paris.
1880	Guy de Maupassant discovers St-Tropez.
1890s	Queen Victoria stays several times in Nice, first at the Grand Hôtel, then later at the Excelsior Régina in Cimiez. Grand Belle Époque hotels are built all along the coast for winter visitors.

20TH- AND 21ST-CENTURY RIVIERA

1912	The Hôtel Carlton opens in Cannes.
1922	The first 'Train Bleu' travels from Calais to the Côte d'Azur.
1923	The summer season is born when the Hôtel du Cap on the Cap d'Antibes stays open in summer for the first time, joined in 1931 by hotels in Cannes.
1942–3	During World War II, the Alpes-Maritimes are occupied by Italian troops and from September 1943 by German troops.
1944	The Liberation of Provence sees landings in the Var.
1946	The first Cannes Film Festival; Picasso installs a studio in the Château Grimaldi in Antibes.
2005	Rainier III dies; Albert II is crowned sovereign prince of Monaco.
2007	Nice tramway opens.
2009	Work begins on a new Cocteau museum in Menton.

WALKS AND TOURS

VIEUX NICE

The labyrinthine streets of Old Nice are where you can discover fine Baroque churches, funky bars and an elegant palace, as well as enjoy lots of foodie treats including the city's best ice cream.

DISTANCE 2.5km (1½ miles)
TIME A full day
START Place Masséna
END Rue Pairolière
POINTS TO NOTE
Most churches and museums in Nice are closed at lunchtime.

Against a backdrop of pastel-coloured houses with green shutters and Baroque churches and campaniles, the picturesque Old Town is a harmonious blend of old and new. It is Nice at its most traditional, where you may find elderly residents who still speak Nissart (an Occitane language related to Provençal) and restaurants serving age-old local specialities, alongside trendy cellar clubs, bohemian bars, art galleries and clothes shops which reflect the young cosmopolitan set who have rejuvenated the district. Behind the tourist-thronged main thoroughfares, there are quiet backstreets and the occasional fine doorway, carved lintel or old *lavoir* (communal wash-house) to discover.

Development

Vieux Nice owes its street plan to the medieval Ville Basse (Lower Town), which grew up at the foot of Colline du Château (Castle Hill, *see p.49*) in the 13th and 14th centuries. It acquired its present appearance in the 16th and 17th centuries when the population of the Ville Haute (Upper Town) was forced down from the citadel and the town was rebuilt with its Baroque churches and communal buildings.

AROUND THE OPÉRA

Begin by the *Fontaine du Soleil* in **place Masséna** *(see pp.34–5)* and enter Vieux Nice along rue de l'Opéra. If you turn right on rue St-François-de-Paule, at no. 24 you will find the now chic **Hôtel Beau Rivage** *(see p.108)*, whose former guests include Nietzsche, Chekhov and Matisse. However, this route turns left, passing the **Hôtel de Ville**, which is a surprisingly inconspicuous building given Nice's usual love of flamboyance. Opposite, at no. 14, **Alziari** (www.alziari.com) draws connoisseurs for its olive oil. A few doors up is the pink-columned **Opéra de Nice** ❶ *(see also p.122)*. A focal point of Nice's cultural scene, it was rebuilt in 1884 on the site of the earlier Théâtre Royal, which was gutted when the stage curtain caught fire. Across the street at no. 7, family-run **Maison Auer** (www.maison-auer.com) has been producing candied fruits and chocolates since 1820.

COURS SALEYA

The street leads into broad **cours Saleya** ❷, where the busy **food and flower market** (Tue–Sun am; flowers all day) and **flea market** (Mon) are held under striped awnings. Frequented by many of the town's best chefs, the food market's laden stalls reflect the sheer profusion and vibrant colour of the Riviera's produce. Bar and restaurant terraces stretch along the sides of the square and waiters do the hard sell to lure customers to their tables, but **Le Safari**, see ⑪①, remains a reliable address, holding out against the chain and theme restaurants.

Above from far left: Opéra and Old Town façades.

Food and Drink

① LE SAFARI

1 cours Saleya; tel: 04 93 80 18 44; daily L and D; €€

This market-side brasserie is a Niçois institution, with a great people-watching terrace. Friendly, high-speed waiters serve up pretty good renditions of local specialities (*salade niçoise*, rabbit and artichoke salad), plus grilled meats and wood-fired pizzas, to an eclectic crowd of locals and tourists.

Place Pierre Gautier

Even better is the part of the market that spills into adjoining **place Pierre Gautier**. Here you are likely to be buying direct from producers, perhaps selling nothing but lemons or bunches of purple artichokes.

On the western side of the square, the **Forum d'Urbanisme et d'Architecture de la Ville de Nice** ❸ (tel: 04 97 13 31 51; Mon–Fri 8.30am–5.30pm, Sat 9am–1pm; free) puts on exhibitions about Nice's architectural heritage and urban projects. Stretching along the square's northern side is the **Palais de la Préfecture**, begun in the 17th century for the Dukes of Savoy, and since 1860 the *préfecture* of the Alpes-Maritimes *département*. The colonnaded façade was added when Nice was briefly returned to the kings of Sardinia-Piedmont after the Revolution.

A little further along cours Saleya is the **Chapelle de la Miséricorde** (Tue 2.30–6pm), which belongs to the Black Penitents, a religious lay fraternity, and is generally considered the finest of all Nice's Baroque interiors.

Rue des Ponchettes

Cross the cours Saleya and head through the arch to rue des Ponchettes, a double alley of low fishermen's cottages, bordered by quai des Etats-Unis on the other side, where the **Galerie des Ponchettes** (tel: 04 93 62 31 24; during exhibitions Tue–Sun 10am–6pm; free) and **Galerie de la Marine** (tel: 04 93 91 92 90; during exhibitions Tue–Sun 10am–6pm; free) are used for exhibitions put on by the municipality.

Ancien Sénat

Return to cours Saleya. At the eastern end is the pedimented building of the **Ancien Sénat**, founded in the early 17th century to administer justice on behalf of the Dukes of Savoy, who were trying to reassert their power in the quasi-independent city. Go past the adjacent Chapelle du St-Suaire (Chapel of the Holy Shroud) and take rue St-Suaire to the **Fashion Gallery**, at no. 5, which sells adventurous clothes and costume jewellery by young designers in a semi-troglodyte boutique carved into the bedrock of Castle Hill.

Right: clock tower of the Palais Rusca on place du Palais.

ÉGLISE STE-RITA

Return along cours Saleya and turn right into rue de la Poissonnerie. On the corner, the **Maison d'Adam et Eve**, one of the oldest buildings in the city, is decorated with a charmingly naïve 16th-century relief of Adam and Eve. Just up the street, the Église de l'Annonciation, more commonly known as **Église Ste-Rita ❹** (daily 7am–noon and 2.30–6.30pm; free), has an unobtrusive exterior that belies the riot of decoration inside. Daylight floods in through a half-dome to reveal six side chapels with a profusion of sculpted saints, barley-sugar columns and sunbursts. This intimate gem is much loved by the Niçois, who light candles in front of the chapel of St Rita, patron saint of lost causes, to the left of the entrance.

RUE DE LA PRÉFECTURE

At the junction with rue de la Préfecture, **Les Distilléries Idéales**, see ⑪②, is a good place for a drink. Take a look also at the **Loggia Communale** of 1574, with its marble arcade, sheltering fragments of columns and sculpture from old buildings. This street is a characteristically Vieux Nice mix, where typically French restaurants, including the acclaimed **Bistrot Antoine**, see ⑪③, give way to a stretch of expat bars where you will not hear a word of French. Also of interest are old-fashioned wine merchant **Caves Caprioglio**

(no. 16); **Ombrelles Bestagno** (no. 17), which has been selling umbrellas and walking sticks since 1850; and **Le Palais d'Osier** (no. 3), which is crammed high with baskets.

PLACE DU PALAIS

The street borders the northern side of **place du Palais**, where the pedimented, white 19th-century **Palais de Justice** (law courts) faces the 1718 clock tower and russet-coloured façade of the Baroque **Palais Rusca**. Go through the gate to the left to see the impressive three-tiered arcades. The square, once the site of a monastery, has a **second-hand book market** on the first and third Saturday of each month.

Food and Drink 🍴

② LES DISTILLÉRIES IDÉALES
24 rue de la Préfecture; tel: 04 93 62 10 66; daily 9am–midnight
A casual place for a drink, along the bar or crowded around tiny pavement tables.

③ BISTROT ANTOINE
27 rue de la Préfecture; tel: 04 93 85 29 57; Tue–Sat L and D; €€
Set amid traditional Vieux Nice bistros, this new-generation bistro has quickly made its mark. It rejuvenates regional dishes and market-inspired plats du jour with refined light presentation and inventive touches. There are well-chosen French regional wines too.

Catherine Ségurane
On place St-Augustin, a plaque pays homage to Catherine Ségurane, the feisty washerwoman credited with saving Nice when besieged by French and Turkish troops in 1543. There are various legends associated with her; one says she seized a Turkish standard on 15 August and pushed back the invaders, holding out until relieved by Emperor Charles V.

Above from left:
Cathédrale Ste-Réparate; place St-François; Palais Communal.

Now head northwards along rue du Marché and rue de la Boucherie. At rue François Gallo, on the left note the **Porte Fausse**, a small stairway that once led to the River Paillon; it now contains an artwork by Sarkis (*b.*1938–) that was created for the arrival of the tramway (*see p.45*).

PLACE DU ROSSETTI

Turn right into rue François Gallo and walk to **place du Rossetti**, the animated heart of the Old Town with flower-hung houses and café terraces.

Cathédrale Ste-Réparate

Dominating the western side is the sculpted façade of the **Cathédrale Ste-Réparate** ❺ (daily 9am–noon and 2–6pm; free); you can just spot the multicoloured tiled dome behind the clock tower. Built on a cruciform plan inspired by St Peter's in Rome in the 1650s, it is dedicated to early Christian virgin martyr, Saint Réparate, the city's patron saint. Her body – accompanied by two angels (hence the name 'Baie des Anges') – is said to have arrived by boat on the shore at Nice after drifting across the Mediterranean from Palestine, where she had been decapitated at the age of 15. The interior, which has preserved most of its original decor, is a grandiose if rather gloomy affair, despite the impressive painted dome over the transept, stucco decoration and a sequence of richly decorated Baroque side chapels, each of which originally belonged to a different wealthy family or town corporation.

Queues leave no doubt, however, as to the square's biggest attraction: the ice creams and sorbets of **Fenocchio**, where over 90 flavours include coffee, rose, beer and lavender.

ÉGLISE DU JÉSUS

Leave the square to the south by rue du Jésus, crossing **place du Jésus**, the location of the popular budget eatery, **Restaurant du Jésus**, see ⑪④, and the Église St-Jacques or **Église du Jésus** ❻ (daily 3–6pm). It was founded by the Jesuit order in 1607 (though the present church dates from 1642–50), and with its single nave and side chapels, defined

---

Route de Baroque

The reconstruction of Vieux Nice in the 1600s coincided with the Catholic Counter-Reformation, which sought a return to the faith after the schism caused by the Reformation. At the forefront was the Jesuit order founded by Ignatius Loyola, whose church of the Gesù in Rome set the model for Nice's Église du Jésus among other churches. Here, decoration takes a didactic role, and brings a new sense of theatre to church architecture to encourage popular piety and the veneration of saints, as well as an expression of the power of the church as seen by its profusion of barley-sugar columns, stripy marble, golden sunbursts and cherubs, and the 'light of God' pouring in through ceiling drums. The Route du Baroque (www.cg06.fr) pinpoints principal Baroque edifices in the Alpes-Maritimes, including Menton, Èze and Villefranche and towns inland.

---

the style of Nice's Counter-Reformation Baroque churches (the blue-and-white classical façade is a later reworking). Inside, the profusion of carved and painted angels and cherubs is striking.

From the church head northwards up rue Droite, once the town's main north–south thoroughfare, and today busy with art galleries and new-agey clothes and trinket shops.

PALAIS LASCARIS

At no. 15, a heavily bossed doorway announces the **Palais Lascaris** ❼ (tel: 04 93 62 72 40; Wed–Mon 10am–noon and 2–6pm; free), the 17th-century Genoese-style mansion of the Lascaris-Ventimille family and Nice's grandest secular Baroque building. The sober street façade does not prepare you for the splendour of the interior, with its magnificent vaulted stairway which is decorated with sculptures and frescoed grotesques. On the second floor, state rooms, with Baroque furniture and tapestries, have spectacular painted ceilings of the mythological scenes *Venus and Adonis*, *The Abduction of Psyche* and *The Fall of Phaeton*, where god and horses tumble from the sky amid a mass of swirling clouds. The first floor houses the municipal collection of 18th- and 19th-century musical instruments. Before leaving, take a look at the period pharmacy by the entrance, with its wooden shelves and faïence drug jars.

PLACE ST-FRANÇOIS

Rue Droite runs into rue St-François and the **place St-François**, home to a small **fish market** (Tue–Sun am) centred around its dolphin fountain. Arcades remain from an earlier cloister, and on one side the 16th-century **Palais Communal** was the seat of town government until 1860.

Continue north along rue Pairolière, a busy shopping street, where foodie temptations include salts and spices at **Girofle et Cannelle** (no. 2) and olives at the **Maison de l'Olive** (no. 18). **L'Escalinada**, see ⑪⑤, is a bastion of Niçois specialities, while at no. 1, customers queue up for plastic plates of *socca*, *pissaladière*, fritters and other Niçois snacks to be eaten at rustic wooden tables at **Chez René Socca**.

Socca

The quintessential Old Town snack is *socca*, a sort of thin, crispy pancake made from chickpea flour and cooked in a large round iron pan. Cut into small portions, it is best served piping hot and seasoned with freshly ground black pepper.

Food and Drink 🍴

④ RESTAURANT DU JÉSUS
1 place du Jésus; tel: 04 93 62 26 46; Mon–Sat L and D; €
Marinated red peppers, home-made gnocchi, pizzas and *petits farcis* are among the rustic fare served at this busy budget joint, although you come here for the raucous atmosphere rather than the cuisine. There are tables out on the square or inside. No credit cards.

⑤ L'ESCALINADA
22 rue Paroilière; tel: 04 93 62 11 71; daily L and D; €
The two whitewashed dining rooms and much-prized terrace are always packed at this Vieux Nice shrine to traditional Niçois specialities, where timeless recipes include *sardines à l'escabèche*, stuffed courgette flowers, gnocchi, ravioli stuffed with *daube de boeuf*, plus a very good lemon meringue tart. No credit cards.

PROMENADE DES ANGLAIS

With its grand hotels and palm trees lining the beach, the legendary promenade des Anglais epitomises elegant Nice. Behind it, the New Town is laid out in a grid of broad avenues and garden squares and offers smart shops and a panoply of 19th- and 20th-century architecture.

> **DISTANCE** 6km (3¾ miles)
> **TIME** A half day
> **START/END** Place Masséna
> **POINTS TO NOTE**
> The promenade des Anglais can get very traffic clogged; all the more reason to explore on foot.

The iconic promenade skirts the Baie des Anges; to the north, modern Nice's architecture is testament to the era when it was *the* place to winter in Europe.

PLACE MASSÉNA

Nice's grandest square and psychological heart, **place Masséna ❶** lies at the crossroads of the north–south avenue Jean Médecin and the old east–west rue de France. It symbolised the town-planning ambitions of the Consiglio d'Ornano (Council of Ornament), which was set up under the King of Sardinia-Piedmont in 1832 to mastermind the expansion of the town west of the River Paillon. A beautiful ensemble of arcaded, deep russet

Above: looking out from the promenade des Anglais across the Baie des Anges.

façades, it was spruced up for the tramway in 2007, with graphic black-and-white paving and a spectacular sculpture by Jaume Plensa *(see p.44)*.

CARRÉ D'OR

Leave the square to the west on pedestrianised rue Masséna; it is tourist central, busy day and night with restaurants and pizzerias. Then take rue Paradis which, along with rue Masséna, avenue de Suède and avenue de Verdun, forms Nice's retail 'Carré d'Or'. Smart clothes shops include preppy Nice-born Façonnable, Max Mara, Chanel, delectable children's clothes at Bonpoint, and designer labels and housewares at Espace Harroch.

Turn right at the end into avenue de Verdun, past jewellers and other high-end stores to the seafront. Here, the modern Hôtel Méridien and glitzy Casino Ruhl, which replaced the Belle Époque casino – still mourned by many today – in the 1970s, mark the start of the promenade des Anglais.

PROMENADE DES ANGLAIS

Sweeping westwards from Jardin Albert 1er along the Baie des Anges, the promenade des Anglais, with its blue chairs, white pergolas, palm trees and grand hotels, has come to symbolise the elegance of Nice; not bad for

something that began in 1822 as an employment exercise. After a harsh winter, local resident Reverend Lewis Way opened a public subscription to construct a footpath linking the Old Town to the growing British colony on the hills further west in a suburb dubbed Newborough. It gained a broad carriageway, pavement and gas lighting in the 1860s, and took on its present appearance in 1931 when the thoroughfare was widened. Despite busy traffic, it still makes a fascinating stroll, with its all-year stream of joggers and rollerbladers and sheer diversity of passers-by.

Palais de la Méditerranée

Just beyond Casino Ruhl, at no. 5, is Nice's main Tourist Office *(see p.105)*. At no. 11, admire the Art Deco façade of the Palais de la Méditerranée ❷, built in 1929 by American millionaire Frank Jay Gould. This symbol of

Naïve Art

The former villa of perfumier François Coty houses the Musée International d'Art Naïf Anatole Jakovsky (avenue Val-Marie; tel: 04 93 71 78 33; Wed–Mon 10am–6pm; free), donated by Romanian art critic Anatole Jakovsky. He was one of the first to admire the colourful, obsessively meticulous works of self-taught, sometimes mentally ill, artists, including Le Douannier Rousseau, Jules Lefranc, Séraphine, Rimbert and Bombois.

Left: shaded view from the promenade.

1930s glamour, with its casino, theatre, art gallery, restaurant and cocktail bar, and its architecture by Charles Delmas and his son Marcel, heralded a new age of modernity. The Palais closed in 1978 and was shamelessly gutted, before reopening as a luxury hotel, apartments and casino.

At no. 27, the pink stucco **Hôtel Westminster** still has its grandiose reception rooms, while **Hôtel West End** (no. 31) was the first of the promenade's grand hotels and opened in 1855.

Musée Masséna

Next door, behind a luscious garden, the recently restored **Musée d'Art et d'Histoire Palais Masséna** ❸ (tel: 04 93 91 19 10; Wed–Mon 10am–6pm; free) was built in 1898 for the grandson of Maréchal Victor Masséna, one of Napoleon's generals. On the ground floor of this interesting museum, a grandiose sequence of reception rooms and a winter garden offer an example of the opulent decorative style of the period, with sumptuous inlaid marquetry, panelling and gilded sphinxes. Upstairs, the collection tells the story of the aristocrats, artists and intellectuals who shaped 19th-century Nice, through an eclectic array of society portraits, paintings, documents, furniture and memorabilia. These include caricatures of Garibaldi, Napoleon's death mask, the cloak worn by Josephine for Napoleon's coronation as King of Naples and paintings of Old Nice. Among the curiosities is a poster in French and Italian calling on citizens to vote in the referendum for Nice to rejoin France on 15 and 16 April 1860.

Beaches

On Nice's long beach, public sections where anyone can stretch out their towel for free alternate with private, pay beaches that are as much about image as swimming and sunbathing, although the sun loungers *(matelas)* are a boon on the uncomfortable pebbles. Castel Plage on quai des États-Unis at the eastern end calls itself 'the beautiful beach for beautiful people' and cultivates its arty reputation with chess matches and art shows; Beau Rivage, belonging to the elegant Vieux Nice hotel, has a vast restaurant serving Med-Asian fusion cuisine; Blue Beach in front of Hôtel West End is a chic dining address by night and child-friendly beach by day, with table tennis, a seawater pool for kids and volleyball; sporty Neptune, opposite the Negresco, has a playground, pedalos, billiards and a pontoon; while trendy Hi Beach is split into lifestyle zones – Play for families, Relax with plants and hammocks, Energy around the bar – plus computers, massages and a restaurant serving contemporary cuisine.

The Negresco

Next to the museum, at no. 37, a sculpture of a jazz trumpeter by Niki de Saint Phalle keeps the frock-coated doormen company under the pink-and-green cupola of **Hôtel Negresco** ❹ *(see p.109)*, Nice's grandest hotel. Built by architect Edouard Niermans, and boasting a glazed *verrière* by Gustave Eiffel over the salon, as well as lavish bathrooms and telephones in the rooms, it was one of the most modern hotels in the world when it opened in 1913. It is worth visiting for a meal at **Le Chantecler** (tel: 04 93 16 64 00; www.hotel-negresco-nice.com) or **La Rotonde**, see ⑪①, or simply for ogling its eccentric mix of grandeur and kitsch. Jeanne Auger, owner since 1958, chooses the decoration herself, mixing antique furniture with canopied beds, and an impressive art collection that ranges from 18th-century portraits by Hyacinthe Rigaud to modern sculptures by Botero and de Saint Phalle.

West along the Promenade

Another extravagant turreted building echos the Negresco on the next corner before the streamlined 1940s and 50s apartments of nos 43–5. At no. 63, a plaque indicates the site of Marie Bashkirtseff's Villa Aquaviva *(see margin, right)*. Next door, at no. 65, the neoclassical **Centre Universitaire Méditerranéen** (tel: 04 97 13 46 10, www.cum-nice.org) was built in the 1930s as a centre of culture and teaching.

Administered by polymath Paul Valéry, whose office has been preserved, it was the precursor of Nice University and today has a busy programme of public lectures, debates and concerts.

MUSÉE DES BEAUX-ARTS

Turn right up rue Paul Valéry and right into rue de France, passing Gloria Mansions – an icon of Art Deco Nice – at no. 125; then cross over and turn left up avenue des Beaumettes. A short cut by the steps on the left brings you out amid the fanciful villas and mock castles of Beaumettes hill, just beneath the **Musée des Beaux-Arts Jules Cheret** ❺ (tel: 04 92 15 28 28; www.musee-beaux-arts-nice.org; Tue–Sun 10am–6pm; free), occupying the palatial villa built for Ukrainian princess Elisabeth Kotschoubey in

---

Food and Drink 🍴

① LA ROTONDE

Hôtel Negresco, 37 promenade des Anglais; tel: 04 93 16 64 00; www.hotel-negresco-nice.com; daily 7am–11.30pm; €€
The Negresco's second restaurant is less formal than the gastronomic Le Chantecler but nevertheless offers elegant cuisine niçoise overseen by the same chef Jean-Denis Rieubland. There's a convenient all-day service in a cheerful fairground setting of merry-go-round horses and musical automatons.

Marie Bashkirtseff
A glittering figure of Nice's Russian colony, painter and diarist Marie Bashkirtseff is remembered for her journal recording high society life in Nice, the Ukraine and Paris – where she studied at the Académie Julian, then one of the few art schools to accept female pupils. Her virtuoso self-portrait in Nice's Musée des Beaux-Arts was painted shortly before she died of tuberculosis in 1884, just before her 26th birthday.

Russian Cathedral

Complete with onion domes, icons and an ornate iconostasis, the Cathédrale Orthodox Russe St-Nicolas (boulevard Tzarewitch; daily 9am–noon, 2.30–6pm (Oct–May until 5pm); charge; *pictured below*) was commissioned in 1912 by Tzarina Maria Feodorovna, mother of Tzar Nicolas II, when Nice's Russian community grew too big for an earlier church on rue Longchamp.

1878, modelled on palaces in St Petersburg. The collection, which has works from the late Middle Ages to the early 20th century, is interesting if rather idiosyncratic, with an emphasis on artists linked to Nice and the south of France.

Ground Floor

Paintings by the early Nice school include saints from an altarpiece attributed to Louis Bréa. There are fine Flemish Mannerist landscapes and 18th-century French and Italian paintings, notably Fragonard's *Head of an Old Man* (undated) and Hubert Robert's picturesque *Gorges d'Ollioules*

(*c.*1783) anticipating Romanticism. The biggest room is devoted to the Van Loo family and dominated by the massive *Theseus Vanquishing the Bull at Marathon* by Carle Van Loo, court painter to Louis XV, who was born in Nice in 1705, and his nephew Louis Michel Van Loo's *Reason Conquering Force*.

First Floor

Up the grand galleried staircase, where group portraits by Nicaise de Keyser depict ancient and modern sages, the first-floor galleries focus on the late 19th and early 20th centuries. Sculpture on the landing includes a bronze of Carpeaux's *Génie de la Danse* (1822) from the Paris Opéra and an original full-scale plaster version of Rodin's *The Kiss* (1886), followed by an assemblage of Impressionist works. There are myriad pastels by Jules Cheret, a pioneering poster artist, plus Marie Bashkirtseff's wonderfully fresh self-portrait, *Autoportrait à la Palette* (1884). A small room is devoted to the strange oils and watercolours by Gustave-Adolphe Mossa, who was the museum's curator from its opening in 1928 to his death in 1971, revealing a personal, rather macabre, vision that mixes Art Nouveau curves and Symbolist angst. Another highlight is a whole room of paintings by Raoul Dufy, where a thickly painted early Fauve view of L'Estaque contrasts with the light brushstrokes and joie de vivre of later scenes of the Riviera.

Above from far left:
three aspects of
the Musée des
Beaux-Arts.

BEHIND THE PROMENADE

Return down avenue des Baumettes, crossing boulevard François Grosso into rue de France. This is the workaday end of the street, with small shops and local bars; note the rare Art Nouveau façade at no. 111. At boulevard Gambetta, you can detour to the **Cathédrale Orthodox Russe** *(see margin, left)*, or turn right into boulevard Victor Hugo, a busy east–west thoroughfare with some fine architecture ranging from classical villas with wrought-iron balconies and a neo-Gothic church, to the incredibly ornate friezes of the **Palais Meyerbeer** (no. 45) and Art Deco mansion blocks.

Quartier des Musiciens

Turn left up avenue Auber in the **Quartier des Musiciens**, with its streets named after composers, which grew following the arrival of the railway in 1861. At place Mozart, a garden square, turn right along rue Rossini. At the end is **Le Bistrot des Viviers**, see ⑪②. Two blocks north along rue Alphonse Karr is the circular façade of the **Grand Escurial** on the left; the former cinema here is now subject of controversial plans to turn it into a supermarket. Walk back down the street, past a breezy 1940s U-shaped apartment complex, to check out some adventurous fashion shops.

Rue de la Buffa

Turn right on rue de la Liberté, crossing place Grimaldi to rue de la Buffa for the 1860s, neo-Gothic **Église Anglicane** (Holy Trinity Anglican Church) at no. 11.

Turn left down rue Dalpozzo, home of **La Cave de l'Origine**, see ⑪③, before heading back along rue de France to place Masséna. On the way, look out for the **Croix de Marbre** ❻; this discreet little shrine, with its cross under a tiled dome, commemorates the meeting in 1538 between François 1er of France, Emperor Charles V and Pope Paul III. It was erected in 1568 on the site of a monastery where the Pope stayed when he was refused accommodation by the inhabitants of Vieux Nice.

CIMIEZ

Smart, residential Cimiez is imbued with the spirit of the Belle Époque and offers glimpses of Nice's Roman past too, but a walk here is also a must for art lovers given its superb museums dedicated to Chagall and Matisse.

DISTANCE 3.25km (2 miles)
TIME A half day
START Former Majestic Hôtel, Boulevard de Cimiez
END Monastère de Cimiez
POINTS TO NOTE
Eating options are very limited in this part of town. It is best to do the walk after lunch or think about bringing a picnic if you intend to make a day of it. Note that the Chagall, Archaeological and Matisse museums are all closed on Tuesday. The start of the tour is easily reached from place Masséna or avenue Jean Médecin via boulevard Dubouchage and avenue Desambrois. If you do not want to return to the town centre on foot, take bus no. 15, 17 or 22 from Arènes–Musée Matisse.

The winding avenues, stucco façades and lush vegetation of Cimiez still evoke the Belle Époque and the era when European aristocracy wintered on the Riviera.

BOULEVARD DE CIMIEZ

Begin at the bottom of **boulevard de Cimiez ❶**. Laid out in the 1880s when olive groves and orchards were sold off as building plots, it threads through the district and is lined with ornate former grand hotels that were built when this was the most fashionable part of town in which to stay. Spot the pink-and-cream former **Grand Hôtel** amid tall palm trees at no. 2, and next door, dating from 1908, the colossal white façade of the **Majestic**, which was once Nice's biggest hotel with 400 bedrooms.

Musée National Marc Chagall
Further along, at the corner with avenue Docteur Ménard, is the **Musée National Marc Chagall ❷** (tel: 04 93 53 87 20; www.musee-chagall.fr; Wed–Mon 10am–6pm; charge), where paintings by Chagall are enhanced to great effect by the low, modern building.

Food and Drink

① CAFÉ DU MUSÉE
Musée National Marc Chagall, avenue Dr Ménard; tel: 04 93 53 87 32; Wed–Mon 10am–6pm; €
Light lunches, teas and snacks are served under the shade of parasols in the pretty Mediterranean garden of the Chagall Museum.

Inaugurated in 1973, the museum was designed in consultation with the artist by André Hermant, a pupil of Le Corbusier, specifically for the artist's paintings on Old Testament themes. In the main room, 12 paintings illustrating episodes from Genesis and Exodus reveal Chagall's ability to mix colour and narrative with a personal iconography.

A smaller gallery to the side contains five dreamlike, rose-tinted paintings of the *Cantiques* (1957–60) on the theme of love, dedicated to his second wife Valentina Brodsky. Other works from the collection are displayed in rotation in temporary exhibitions. Be sure to visit the auditorium, where there are three intensely coloured stained-glass windows and related studies depicting *The Creation of the World*. The **Café du Musée**, see ⓕ①, is a good place for refreshments.

Grandes Residences

Return to boulevard de Cimiez, where across the street, **Villa Paradisio**, built for Baronne Hélène de Rothschild, now belongs to the town's education service, but is surrounded by a pretty public garden. Set back in gardens at no. 46, the former **Hôtel Alhambra**, with its two mosque-like minarets, and neighbouring **Villa Ellard** are two rare examples of Moorish taste. The former **Riviera Palace** at no. 39 and **Winter Palace** at no. 82 were both designed by Charles Delmas, architect of the Carlton in Cannes.

After the **Palace Prince de Galles** at no. 53, detour left along boulevard Prince de Galles to the fanciful mock medieval **gateway ❸** of **Campus Valrose**. The neo-Gothic Château Valrose itself (the main entrance is on avenue de Valrose), built in 1867 for a Russian noble, is now part of Nice University's Science Faculty and is out of bounds, but you can visit the park which sprawls over the hillside, with a waterfall, lake and an authentic Russian wooden *isba* (house) transported from Odessa.

Hôtel Excelsior Régina

Return to boulevard de Cimiez. At the junction with avenue de la Reine Victoria, a sentimental white marble statue portrays Queen Victoria accepting flowers from figures symbolising towns

p.43

Nice Jazz Festival
Held each July in the Roman arena and in the Parc des Arènes, Nice Jazz Festival (tel: 04 95 04 95 50; www.nicejazzfestival. fr) adopts a wide definition of jazz, from modern jazz and big band to electro-jazz, blues and rock. Regularly featuring some of the very best names from America, it is renowned for its relaxed mood as the audience picnics and promenades between three different stages.

Above from left:
Roman excavations by the Musée Archéologique; viewing artworks at the Musée Matisse.

on the Riviera. Crowning the boulevard behind, the ornate **Hôtel Excelsior Régina** ❹ was designed by architect Sébastien-Marcel Biasini in 1896, in anticipation of a visit by Queen Victoria, who stayed here three times under the name of Lady Balmoral and visited the town in a trap pulled by a donkey. The royal retinue, including grooms, ladies in waiting and Indian servants, occupied the entire west wing with a suite of over 70 rooms, commemorated by the crown over the entrance. The hotel was requisitioned as a military hospital during World War I and following the crash of 1929 was converted into apartments, two of which were bought by Matisse, who lived here at the end of his life, sketching on the ceiling from his bed with a brush attached to a long pole.

Grand Hotels

While earlier visitors built themselves villas or rented those of their peers, by the late 19th century, when the winter season meant that being next to the sea was not that important but great views of it were, hilly Cimiez's grand hotels became the place to stay; a reputation confirmed by the arrival of Queen Victoria in the 1890s. The palatial new buildings, many financed by banker Henri Germain, founder of the Société Foncière Lyonnaise, offered modern comforts, such as lifts, private bathrooms and hot running water, as well as the space to keep a retinue of servants. The crash of 1929, the birth of the summer season in the 1930s and the desire to be next to the sea sealed the decline of Cimiez's grand hotels. They closed one by one to be divided up into apartments; nevertheless, the grand Belle Époque architecture remains.

REMAINS OF ROMAN NICE

Across the boulevard, at the **Arènes de Cimiez** ❺, you suddenly leap back 2,000 years to the Roman city of Cemenelum, founded in the 1st century AD as a military staging post on the Via Aurelia and subsequently capital of the Imperial province of Alpes Maritimae. The amphitheatre itself, of which only a few tiers of seats and a couple of entrance tunnels remain, is disappointing compared to the much larger, better-preserved amphitheatres at Arles, Nîmes and Fréjus, although it makes a pleasant venue for the Nice Jazz Festival *(see margin, p.41)*.

Musée Archéologique

You get a much better idea of the importance of Cemenelum in the adjacent **Musée Archéologique** ❻ (160 avenue des Arènes de Cimiez; tel: 04 93 81 59 57; Wed–Mon 10am–6pm; free) and archaeological site. Start with the museum, which has displays of statues, glassware and jewellery on the ground floor and sarcophagi and inscribed stelae, as well as the chance to try out Roman boardgames, in the basement. Exit the other side to visit the outdoor excavations, where extensive remains include imposing walls and bits of hypocaust from three bathing establishments that date from the settlement's 3rd-century heyday; traces of streets and shops; and a 5th-century paleo-Christian church and baptistry.

MUSÉE MATISSE

Behind the ruins, you can spot the rust-coloured **Musée Matisse ❼** (164 avenue des Arènes, tel: 04 93 81 08 08; www.musee-matisse-nice.org; Wed–Mon 10am–6pm; free), which is reached via the **Parc des Arènes**, a lovely grove of olive trees and a good place to picnic. The extensive collection spans the artist's entire career, and demonstrates how he assimilated such inspirations as Riviera sunlight, patterned textiles, classical sculpture and his voyages to North Africa and Tahiti. Highlights include Fauve portrait, small oil studies for different versions of *La Danse*, *Odalesque au Coffret Rouge* (1926), a series of small bronze heads of Jeannette, virtuoso drawing; and the 8m- (26ft-) long, cut-out *Fleurs et Fruits* (1953), which provides a ripple of colour across the atrium gallery.

CIMETIÈRE DE CIMIEZ

Leave the park by the steps on the eastern side to **place du Monastère de Cimiez**, opposite the garish façade of the Franciscan church. To the left of the church enter **Cimetière de Cimiez ❽**, burial place for many British and Russian aristocrats, and follow signs to the left to pay further homage to Matisse at the simple tomb that sits on its own terrace in the gardens below. Painter Raoul Dufy is buried on the opposite side of the cemetery.

Église Franciscain

From Dufy's tomb, follow the path through a small gate into the rose garden from where you can admire the view, including the domed **observatory** (designed by Charles Garnier and Gustave Eiffel), before visiting the early-Gothic **Église Franciscain ❾** (Mon–Sat 10am–noon and 3–6pm; free). The draw here is the collection of three paintings – a *Pièta* triptych (*c.*1475), *Crucifixion* (1512) and *Deposition* (*c.*1520) – by Louis Bréa, the leading figure in a dynasty of Nice artists, which show his development of style.

In the adjoining **Monastère Notre-Dame de Cimiez**, a small **museum** (hours as above) presents the history of the Franciscan order in Nice.

Matisse in Nice

Henri Matisse first came to Nice in 1917 when he stayed at Hôtel Beau Rivage in Vieux Nice and visited Renoir in Cagnes-sur-Mer. From the 1920s, he divided his time between Paris, Nice (living first on place Charles Félix and later at the Excelsior Régina) and Vence *(see p.72)*. His paintings and cut-outs at that time were heavily influenced by the strong light and colours of the Riviera.

PROMENADE DES ARTS

The landscaped promenade between Vieux Nice and the New Town is a focus for the arts and daring modern architecture, with plenty of public art to enjoy and the city's new gallery district to explore.

De l'Art

To find out what's on in the art world, pick up the foldout brochure *De l'Art* (www. de-lart.org) for a programme of contemporary art shows and openings in Nice and across the Alpes-Maritimes region.

Villa Arson

For Nice's most adventurous art shows, head to Villa Arson, Centre National d'Art Contemporain (20 avenue Stéphen Liégeard; tel: 04 92 07 73 73; www.villa-arson.org; Wed–Mon 2–6pm; free) in the north of the city, a unique combination of an art school and exhibition space in a 17th-century Italianate villa, largely disguised by a radical raw concrete and pebble extension.

DISTANCE 4km (2½ miles)
TIME A half day
START Jardin Albert 1er
END Théâtre de la Photographie et de l'Image
POINTS TO NOTE
On Mondays, the Mamac and the Théâtre de la Photographie et de l'Image are closed; most of the private art galleries are also only open Tuesday to Saturday.

Running like a border between Vieux Nice and the New Town, the promenade du Paillon was created when the River Paillon was covered over for public health reasons in the 1800s. Today it has become a 'river of culture', where gardens and cultural buildings alternate with outdoor sculptures.

JARDIN ALBERT 1ER

Enter the **Jardin Albert 1er** ❶ from avenue de Verdun. Despite busy traffic along the seafront the meandering paths, palms trees and iron bandstand still have a blowsy, pleasure-garden feel. In the centre, the **Théâtre de Verdure**

amphitheatre is used for outdoor concerts in summer. Towards place Masséna, admire Bernar Venet's massive 19m- (62ft-) high painted steel *Arc 115°5* – one of a series of arcs the French sculptor has made since the 1960s that are designed according to mathematical formulae – which seems almost to float over the lawn.

PLACE MASSÉNA

Place Masséna *(see also p.34)* is Nice's elegant centrepiece and, since the arrival of the tramway in 2007 *(see margin, right)*, is also the setting for an art installation, **Conversation à Nice** ❷, by Spanish artist Jaume Plensa. Seven resin figures squatting atop tall metal poles, symbolising a dialogue between continents, are eerily white by day and illuminated from within in a subtly evolving colourful glow at night. At the same time, the **Fontaine du Soleil** ❸ (Sun Fountain), with bronze sculptures by Alfred Janniot representing the planets, was returned to the southern side of the square after restoration. It appears without the vast nude statue of Apollo that crowned it when it first went up in 1956.

PROMENADE DES ARTS

Continue along the promenade du Paillon. After Lycée Masséna on the left, make a short detour left to 8 rue Désiré Niel, where the gallery **Atelier Soardi ④** (tel: 04 93 62 32 03; www.soardi.fr) occupies a disused film studio rented by Matisse from 1930–3 to paint his vast composition *La Danse* for American collector Dr Alfred Barnes.

Return to the promenade du Paillon, taking steps up onto the esplanade of the **promenade des Arts**, which was created in the 1980s by mayor Jacques Médecin as part of his ambitious cultural programme.

Architects Yves Bayard and Henri Vidal's carrara marble complex comprises the octagonal **Théâtre National de Nice** *(see p.123)*, which is renowned for premiering new drama, the Musée d'Art Moderne et Contemporain, better known as Mamac *(see p.46)*, and the **sculpture terrace** between the two, where a *Stabile* by Calder, Borovsky's

Above from far left: *Fontaine du Soleil* in Place Masséna; view from Mamac.

Tramway Artworks
In what Nice describes as 'the largest open-air museum in France', works by 15 international artists are dotted along the 9km (6 miles) of tramway and have renewed the city's image as a centre of creation. The journey itself is part of the art experience, with specially designed station signs and specially designed audio announcements inside the tram. There are guided visits of the tramway's artworks in English and French every Friday at 7pm; reserve at the Tourist Office (08 92 70 74 07; www.nicetourisme. com; charge).

École de Nice

In the late 1950s and 60s, Nice shot to the forefront of the French art scene, thanks to the trio Yves Klein, Arman and Martial Raysse, who were championed by critic Pierre Restany, and later joined by César, Sosno, Ben, Niki de Saint Phalle and Robert Malaval. Although associated with Nouveau Réalisme (the French equivalent of Pop Art), Fluxus and Supports-Surfaces, the École de Nice was as much about energy and a sometimes anarchist attitude as a stylistic school.

Below: *Tête Carrée*.

Man with a Suitcase and Niki de Saint Phalle's *Loch Ness Monster* fountain, part of a huge donation by the artist to the city in 2001, prepare the way for the art to come.

Mamac

While the **Musée d'Art Moderne et Contemporain ❺** (Modern and Contemporary Art Museum, tel: 04 97 13 42 01; www.mamac-nice.org; Tue–Sun 10am–6pm; free) focuses on art from 1960 to the present, the museum's strength lies in its holding of the École de Nice *(see margin, left)*, which is pitted against an excellent representation of parallel movements in American Pop Art, including Warhol, Lichtenstein and Johns, and abstraction by artists such as Frank Stella and Ellsworth Kelly, along with varied temporary exhibitions.

An entire room is devoted to the pivotal figure of Yves Klein, who reconciled conceptual ideas and performances with a visual sensibility, evident in his trademark IKB (International Klein Blue) canvases and sculptures and *anthropométries*, where female models covered in paint were rolled like a living paintbrush over the canvas. Other rooms contain Arman's accumulations and cut-up musical instruments, Jacquet's *Déjeuner sur l'Herbe* and an exceptional donation by Niki de Saint Phalle.

Leaving the museum on the eastern side, cross the street to **Galerie Depardieu** (64 boulevard Risso; tel: 04 97 12 12 97; www.galerie-depar dieu.com; Mon–Fri 9.30am–12.30pm and 2.30–6.30pm, Sat by appointment), a dynamic young gallery, which mixes art shows with a programme of live jazz and readings.

Tête Carrée

Continue north, where you cannot miss the *Tête Carrée* ❻ (Square Head) a 30m- (98ft-) high grey head that morphs into a cube (in fact the offices of the Bibliothèque Louis Nucéra, which is itself hidden underground). It is described by its creator, sculptor Sacha Sosno, as an 'inhabited sculpture' and its giant chin looks rather menacing when seen from underneath.

Acropolis Centre de Congrès

Next cross rue Barla to the **Acropolis Centre de Congrès ❼** (1 esplanade J.F. Kennedy), a conference centre and concert hall, which sits behind landscaped fountains. Although now due for a face-lift, the building by Nice architects Buzzi, Bernasconi and Baptiste was considered one of the most beautiful congress centres in Europe when it opened in 1984, and integrates artworks both inside and out. By the main entrance is Arman's *Music Power*, a monumental bronze pile of sliced-up cellos.

Continue walking around the building past the bowling alley and arts cinema **Cinémathèque de Nice** *(see p.122)* for Noël Dolla's steel cut-out *Les Trois Mondes*.

Above from far left:
Mamac artworks.

GALLERY DISTRICT

Walk back towards Mamac along avenue Gallieni and turn right into rue Defly. This part of the New Town, largely undiscovered by tourists, is home to a burgeoning gallery district, where contemporary art galleries mix with antiquarian booksellers, unusual design shops and laid-back bars and bistros. On the corner, **RDF Galerie** (2 rue Defly; 04 93 98 12 75; www.rdf galerie.com; Tue–Sat 3–7.30pm, July and Aug by appointment) features young artists in a variety of media, from painting to video installations to collaborations with DJs. A couple of doors up at no. 6, **Galerie Helenbeck** (04 93 54 22 82; www.galeriehelenbeck.fr; Tue and Thur–Sat 2–7.30pm) specialises in graffiti art and photography along with unusual artist-decorated furniture.

Turn left into rue Gioffredo and then right into rue Delille, perhaps stopping for a meal at **Le Gloss**, see ⑪①. At the end of the street turn left into boulevard Dubouchage, passing the **Villa Rambourg** (at no. 21bis), now a library of antiquarian books, posters and postcards, which has an attractive public garden at the rear.

Théâtre de la Photographie et de l'Image

At no. 27, behind a streamlined Moderne façade, the **Théâtre de la Photographie et de l'Image ❽** (tel: 04 97 13 42 20; www.tpi-nice.org; Tue–Sun 10am–6pm; free) puts on excellent photography exhibitions in the former premises of the ornately decorated Cercle Artistique, a gentleman's club founded to promote Niçois writers and artists. There are a couple of good places to eat nearby: try **Aphrodite**, see ⑪②, for exciting modern cuisine, or **L'Instant T**, see ⑪③, for light meals.

If you want to extend the tour, continue along boulevard Dubouchage and turn right into avenue Jean Médecin for the Nice-Étoile tram stop to discover Nice's ambitious tramway art project *(see margin, p.45)*.

Food and Drink 🍴

① LE GLOSS
16 rue Delille; tel: 04 93 81 71 87; www.le-gloss.fr; Mon–Fri L and D, Sat D only; €
This sleek, artily lit designer eatery is very popular with laid-back young Niçois for lunch or an after work aperitif. The easy-going menu takes in gnocchi, plates of *farcis*, steaks and global faves like fajitas.

② APHRODITE
10 boulevard Dubouchage; tel: 04 93 85 63 53; www.restaurant-aphrodite.com; Tue–Sat L and D; €€
In this dressy restaurant with a sophisticated dining room and lush garden terrace, chef David Faure's beautifully presented modern Mediterranean cooking is an inventive personal blend of tradition and fashionable touches. In the evening there is also a more revolutionary 'techno-émotionelle' menu using modern molecular techniques.

③ L'INSTANT T
35 boulevard Dubouchage; tel: 04 93 85 13 50; Mon–Sat 7.30am–7pm; €
Salads, omelettes, hamburgers and savoury tarts are served all day at this stylish little café-cum-tea room, which has tables outside in a prettily planted front garden.

COLLINE DU CHÂTEAU AND VIEUX PORT

Now a pleasant park, Colline du Château (Castle Hill) bears the traces of medieval Nice. It sits above the site where the Niçois' prehistoric ancestors first settled and the city's picturesque port and antiques district.

Midday Cannon

Every noon, a cannon shot fired from Colline du Château resounds over the town. This tradition was inaugurated by Sir Thomas Coventry-More in the 1860s to ensure that his forgetful wife returned home in time to prepare lunch, and was perpetuated by the municipality from 1871.

DISTANCE 6km (3¾ miles)

TIME A half day

START/END Place Garibaldi

POINTS TO NOTE

Colline du Château can also be reached by lift from the eastern end of Quai des États-Unis (daily summer 9.30am–7pm, winter 10am–5.30pm; charge) up to Tour Bellanda. This walk can be combined with Vieux Nice (see p.28); for a picnic, stock up at cours Saleya market before climbing the steps at the eastern end of rue Rossetti, then turn left on Montée du Château to reach the cemeteries.

For centuries, Colline du Château was the heart of medieval Nice, which grew up around the castle, before the population moved down to the coastal plain. Today, nothing remains of the citadelle, but the park laid out in its place provides a shady interlude on hot summer days and plenty of gorgeous views over the bay and the Old Town.

PLACE GARIBALDI

Start at **place Garibaldi** ❶, the beautiful arcaded square, built in 1782–92 by King Victor-Amédée III of Sardinia as a regal entrance to the city on the new road from Turin. Originally called piazza Victoria, it was later renamed after the Nice-born hero of Italian reunification, whose statue stands in the middle. On the southwestern side, the **Grand Café de Turin**, see , is known for its seafood. Next to it, rue Neuve – a quiet backstreet surprisingly undisturbed by the tourist throng nearby – leads into Vieux Nice. Continue along rue de la Providence to place Ste-Claire, where the **Chapelle de la Visitation** ❷ has a remarkable trompe l'oeil façade.

Food and Drink

① GRAND CAFÉ DE TURIN

5 place Garibaldi; tel: 04 93 62 29 52; Thur–Tue 8am–10pm; €€

This seafood brasserie has been shucking oysters for over a century, drawing a faithful Niçois clientele despite a sometimes grouchy service. The speciality is lavish platters of *fruits de mer*, where oysters, crabs and prawns are accompanied by some rarer treats, such as *violets* (sea potatoes) and *oursins* (sea urchins) in winter.

COLLINE DU CHÂTEAU

Through the gate to the left, Escalier Ménica Rondelly zigzags up the hillside bringing you out beside the **Cimetière Catholique ❸**, full of winged angels, tragic maidens and other funerary monuments to Niçois notables. Next to it, towards the sea is the **Cimetière Israelite** (Jewish Cemetery) with its funerary stelae. From here, the road climbs up to **Parc du Château ❹**, with magnificent views along the way. Follow the sound of water up to the **Cascade**, which was built in the 19th century on the site of the medieval keep, using water diverted from the River Vésubie. Steps around the rear lead to an outdoor amphitheatre, used in summer for *La Castillada*, a promenade-spectacle recounting the history of Nice.

Medieval Ruins

Below, a fenced-off **archaeological site ❺** protects the fragmentary ruins of the Romanesque cathedral and bits of houses which, though poorly labelled, give some idea of the medieval residential district destroyed in the siege of 1691. Follow the path to the

Above from far left: looking out from Colline du Château; view across town to Mamac.

southwestern corner overlooking the sea to the solid round **Tour Bellanda** , a mock fortification reconstructed in the 19th century; Hector Berlioz stayed here in 1844. You can descend by a **lift** (daily summer 9.30am–7pm, winter 10am–5.30pm; charge), which occupies the well shaft dug in the 16th century to supply water to the citadelle, or by the footpath that zigzags down to quai des États-Unis.

MONUMENT AUX MORTS

At the bottom turn left on quai Rauba Capeu – Nissart for 'flying hat' because of the breeze – to the powerful **Monument aux Morts** **❼**, which commemorates the 4,000 Niçois killed in World War I. Elongated Modernist allegorical sculptures by Alfred Janniot

of War (symbolised by figures of Liberty, Strength, Sacred Fire and Victory) face Peace (symbolised by Labour, Love of Home and Fecundity) on either side of a colonnaded temple.

VIEUX PORT

Just beyond on place Guynemar, a statue of Sardinian king Charles Félix points his finger out to sea over the **Vieux Port**, which despite its name was actually excavated only in the late 18th century (previously, fishing boats were simply pulled up on the shore and Nice's main port was at nearby Villefranche-sur-Mer). Today, big yachts and gin palaces moor along the western quay, **quai Lunel**, while tiny wooden *pointu* fishing boats can still be seen along the eastern side.

You might want to pause at the **Marché aux Puces** (Tue–Sat 10am–6pm) on quai Lunel, source of diverse bric-a-brac and collectables. Across the street at **Confiserie Florian** (14 quai Papacino; tel: 04 93 55 43 50; www.confiserieflorian.com; daily 9am–noon and 2–6.30pm), you can watch chocolates being made downstairs before going up to the boutique; violet- and rose-flavour chocolates are particular specialities.

Place Ile de Beauté was constructed following Genoese fashion – with arcaded ground floor, deep-red façades and ornate trompe l'oeil window frames – along the northern side of the port in the 1780s. Halfway along, the

Historic Hill

For such an inconspicuous bit of rock, Colline du Château has seen a lot of history. Settled in the 10th century BC by Ligurian tribes, Greek Nikaia grew up on its flank and during the Dark Ages the population took refuge here from barbarian invasions. By the 11th century, a keep stood on the highest point and a walled town with churches, monasteries, a market and noble residences emerged. Following the siege of Nice in 1543, when the hill held out against allied French and Turkish troops, Duke Emmanuel Philibert I decided to construct a powerful citadel, forcing the townspeople down to the plain. The Upper Town's fate was sealed when Nice was besieged again in 1691, and in 1706 a victorious Louis XIV razed the citadel. It was transformed into a public park in the 1820s.

sailors' church, **Église Notre-Dame du Port** (tel: 04 93 89 53 05; Mon–Sat 9–11.30am and 3–5.30pm, Sun 9–11.30am), stands out for the purity of its neoclassical style, with ribbed columns and coffered ceiling.

Musée de Paléontologie Humaine de Terra Amata

Before continuing around the port, detour to 25 boulevard Carnot to the curious yet fascinating **Musée de Paléontologie Humaine de Terra Amata** (entrance on Impasse Terra Amata; tel: 04 93 55 59 93; www.musee-terra-amata.org; Tue–Sun 10am–6pm; free). It is located at the bottom of an apartment block on the very spot, discovered in 1966, where a tribe of elephant hunters briefly camped on the beach 400,000 years ago when the sea level was 26m (85ft) higher than today. The centrepiece is a large cast of the site, showing traces of tools, animal bones and even a footprint left behind, while the upstairs mezzanine explains the lifestyle of these prehistoric nomadic hunters with displays of axeheads, flint tools and a reconstructed hut.

Boulevard Franck Pilatte

Double back to the port, where the eastern quay, **quai des Deux Emmanuel**, is lined with fish restaurants and bars, such as **Ma Nolan's**, see ⑪②, and **L'Ane Rouge**, see ⑪③. Take the stairs at the end up to **boulevard Franck Pilatte**, popular with locals for a promenade or for a swim from the rocks, without the crowds of the main beaches off the promenade des Anglais. Look out for attractive twin villas Castor and Pollux on the left, and the castle-like Château d'Anglais on Mont Boron in the distance, built by English military engineer Robert Smith in 1857; and watch kids divebombing into the sea from the high board just before chic restaurant La Réserve.

ANTIQUES DISTRICT

Return to place Ile de Beauté, continuing straight on into rue Antoine Gauthier. Here, and on adjoining rue Catherine Ségurane, it is fun to browse the 100 or so **antiques dealers** clustered behind the port (www.nice-antic.fr) before returning to place Garibaldi.

Watersports

On the eastern edge of the port at 50 boulevard Franck Pilatte, the Base Nautique is home to assorted sailing, rowing and diving clubs and schools. Founded in 1883, the Club Nautique de Nice (tel: 04 93 89 39 78; www.cnnice.org) has sailing and rowing sections (keen oarsman Matisse was a member in the 1920s) and runs courses for children and adults. The Aigle Nautique (tel: 04 93 56 77 99; http://aiglenautique.free.fr) is an umbrella group of seven diving clubs.

Food and Drink 🍴

② MA NOLAN'S

5 quai des Deux Emmanuel; tel: 04 93 80 23 87; www.ma-nolans.com; daily L and D; €

This sophisticated Irish bar draws a French and international clientele for drinks and pub grub, either outside on the terrace or inside the woody interior where sports events are screened on television and live bands play most nights. Salads, sandwiches and burgers are served all day.

③ L'ANE ROUGE

7 quai des Deux Emmanuel; tel: 04 93 89 49 63; www.anerougenice.com; Fri–Tue L and D, Thur D; €€€

At the dressiest of the portside restaurants, chef Michel Devillers serves up inventive starters and more classic mains, with an emphasis on fish. Service is excellent though rather formal, and there is a good-value lunch menu.

CORNICHES DRIVE

The three Corniche coast roads abound in scenic views and offer exclusive residential peninsulas, Belle Époque resorts, Roman ruins and picturesque medieval hill villages along the way.

DISTANCE 43km (27 miles)

TIME One day if doing a loop back to Nice; two or three days if combined with the Monaco and Menton tours, *see pp.58–69*

START Vieux Port, Nice

END Èze Village

POINTS TO NOTE

This tour follows sections of all three parallel Corniche roads: the Basse (Lower) Corniche D6098, Moyenne (Middle) Corniche D6007 and Grande (Upper) Corniche D2564. The Basse and Moyenne Corniches have recently been renumbered, but you may still find road signs and maps indicating the N98 and N7. Part of this tour could be done by public transport; frequent trains between Nice and Menton stop at Villefranche-sur-Mer, Beaulieu-sur-Mer and Cap d'Ail. Note that Èze station is at Èze-Bord-du-Mer and not Èze Village; similarly, the nearest station for Roquebrune Village is Carnolès, followed by a steep uphill footpath.

East towards the Italian border, the white limestone Pre-Alps fall almost directly into the sea, creating some of the Riviera's most dramatic settings and exclusive peninsulas.

BASSE CORNICHE

From place Ile de Beauté on the Vieux Port, take boulevard Carnot (D6098), start of the Basse Corniche. This climbs eastwards from Nice around the suburb of Mont Boron; the villas along it get more extravagant as you go.

Villefranche–sur–Mer

After about 5km (3 miles) the road reaches **Villefranche-sur-Mer ❶**. Although now mainly a place for a

Food and Drink 🍴

① LE COSMO

11 place Amélie Pollonnais, Villefranche-sur-Mer; tel: 04 93 01 84 05; daily L and D; €€

This friendly modern brasserie and cocktail bar has a big terrace overlooking the Cocteau Chapel and is good for inventive salads, steak tartare, pasta or catch of the day. Food is served all day in summer.

meal out for the Niçois and a stop for cruise ships, it was founded as a *ville-franche* (customs free port) by the Counts of Provence. For centuries, it was the main port of the Comté de Nice – and after World War II until the 1960s, a US naval base – thanks to its natural deep-water harbour.

Turn right off the Corniche, fork left down avenue Sadi Carnot and park on place Wilson between the Citadelle and the Port de la Santé.

Overlooking the harbour, where a few *pointu* fishing boats still sell their catch direct, is the medieval **Chapelle St-Pierre** (tel: 04 93 76 90 70; summer Tue–Sun 10am–noon and 3–7pm, winter Tue–Sun 10am–noon and 2–6pm, closed mid-Nov–mid-Dec; charge). Often simply called the **Cocteau Chapel**, it was decorated with frescoes of the life of St Peter, patron saint of fishermen and slightly risqué images of fishing folk by poet, artist and film-maker Jean Cocteau *(see also p.66)* in 1957–8. Cocteau was a frequent guest at the Hôtel Welcome next door.

Up a few steps, **place Amélie Pollonais** is home to a flea market on Sundays, a crafts market on Mondays in summer and the pleasant brasserie **Le Cosmo**, see ⑪①. Beyond the chapel, **quai Courbet** is lined with

Above from far left: seaside fun at Villefranche-sur-Mer; view of Villefranche from Villa Ephrussi de Rothschild.

fish restaurants, including venerable **La Mère Germaine**, see ⑪②.

Go through Portail de Robert to **rue Obscure**, which runs parallel to the quayside. This atmospheric, covered street dates from the 13th century and once sheltered townsfolk when the town came under attack; it is also where Cocteau filmed part of *Orphée* (1950). At the western end, climb stepped rue de l'Église to the 18th-century **Église St-Michel** (daily, hours vary). In front of the altar to the left of the main altar is a 17th-century wood sculpture of the Dead Christ carved from a single block of figwood; the church also has a fine organ sometimes used for concerts.

Back at place Wilson, on the western side, the massive **Citadelle** (June–Sept 10am–noon and 3–6.30pm, Sun 2–6.30pm, Oct–May 10am–noon and

Below: details from the flora in the gardens of Villa Ephrussi de Rothschild.

2–5.30pm, Sun 1.30–5.30pm; free) was built in 1557 by the Duke of Savoie to protect the town after the port had been occupied by Barbarossa's Turkish fleet in 1543. It now contains the Town Hall, a congress centre and four minor museums: the **Musée Volti**, with voluptuous female sculptures by Antoniucci Volti; the modern painting collection of **Musée Goetz-Boumeester**; a room devoted to the regiment of Chasseurs-Alpins; and the **Collection Roux**, displaying model scenes of medieval life.

St-Jean-Cap-Ferrat

Return to the D6098, then shortly after, take the D25 right towards St-Jean-Cap-Ferrat, a millionaires' enclave. A side road turns left to **Villa Ephrussi de Rothschild ❷** (tel: 04 93 01 33 09; www.villa-ephrussi.com; daily Feb–Oct 10am–6pm, July–Aug 10am–7pm, Nov–Jan Mon–Fri 2–6pm, Sat, Sun and school hols 10am–6pm; charge). The pink-and-white Italianate villa was built between 1905–12 for Béatrice Ephrussi, daughter of banker Baron Alphonse de Rothschild and wife of another wealthy banker Maurice Ephrussi, and an avid collector who filled her home with beautiful *objets*, including medieval and Rennaisance art, Gobelins tapestries, Vincennes and Sèvres porcelain and ceilings by Tiepolo. The highlight, however, is the themed gardens, complete with musical fountains, exotic cactuses, romantic roses and medieval statuary.

Walking the Caps

The best way to get to see the Riviera's exclusive headlands is along the Sentier du Littoral (Coastal Footpath). At Cap Ferrat, the path goes from the Plage Passable past the lighthouse around the end of the Cap beneath the gardens of the luxurious Grand Hôtel du Cap Ferrat to Port St-Jean. At Cap d'Ail, the path runs between Plage Mala and Plage Marquet. On Cap Martin (between Monaco and Menton) take the Sentier des Douaniers (Customs Officers' Footpath) from Roquebrune station to Carnolès via the Mangano beach and Le Corbusier's *cabanon* (cabin; tel: 04 93 35 62 87; Tue and Fri at 10am, must be reserved in advance); there are several places where you can bathe directly from the rocks.

Return to the D25, which loops round the peninsula; soon after, to the right, a side road descends to the small but pleasant **Plage Passable**. Just beyond this turning on the right spot the gateway of **Villa les Cèdres**, the former residence of King Léopold II of Belgium. The road passes through **St-Jean-Cap-Ferrat**, which consists essentially of a yachting marina and some upmarket restaurants, such as **La Voile d'Or**, see ⑪③, as well as **Plage Paloma**, another decent small public beach on the headland east of the Port along avenue Jean Mermoz.

Beaulieu-sur-Mer

The D25 continues along the seafront. Once a fashionable winter resort for crowned heads, palmy **Beaulieu-sur-Mer** has a sedate feel, with its pink Belle Époque casino, yacht harbour, grand hotels and gorgeous Rotunda building. On the waterfront, the **Villa Grecque Kérylos** ❸ (impasse Gustave Eiffel; tel: 04 93 01 47 29; www.villa-kerylos.com; daily Feb–Oct 10am–6pm, July–Aug 10am–7pm, Nov–Jan Mon–Fri 2–6pm, Sat, Sun and school hols 10am–6pm; charge) is an idealised reconstruction of a Greek villa, inspired by 2nd-century BC villas of the island of Delos and built between 1902–8 for wealthy German scholar Theodor Reinach. It is decorated with meticulous reproductions of antique statues, frescoes, mosaics and antique furniture, as well as the necessary mod cons of the day.

Back on the Basse Corniche, Beaulieu merges into the seaside sprawl of Èze-Bord-de-Mer, from where you can glimpse Èze Village *(see p.57)* high up on the cliff.

Cap d'Ail

Some 7km (4½ miles) to the east, **Cap d'Ail** ❹ is at first sight an ungainly residential satellite for people who work in Monaco. Turn right off the main road, however, to discover Belle Époque gems, such as **Villa Lumière**, residence of the film pioneer brothers, and the **former Eden Palace hotel**, now apartments. To the right of the latter, a footpath leads down to **Plage Mala**, one of the Riviera's most beautiful beaches, with little shacks, trendy Eden restaurant and gorgeous views of the bay and mountains above.

Above from far left:
Villa Ephrussi de Rothschild; Beaulieu-sur-Mer's casino.

Food and Drink

② LA MÈRE GERMAINE
9 quai Courbet, Villefranche-sur-Mer; tel: 04 93 01 71 39; www.meregermaine.com; Christmas–mid-Nov daily L and D; €€€
Run by the same family since 1938, the most famous of the string of restaurants along the harbour (Cocteau was a regular) is a dressy place, known for its fine fish and shellfish.

③ LA VOILE D'OR
Port de Plaisance, 7 avenue Jean Mermoz, St-Jean-Cap-Ferrat; tel: 04 93 01 13 13; Easter–mid-Oct daily L and D; €€€€
This smart restaurant overlooking the pretty harbour of St-Jean has been rejuvenated in the hands of chef Georges Pélissier, who has worked at some of the Riviera's best restaurants including Byblos and the Juana.

Just beyond Èze
railway station, the
Sentier Frédéric
Nietzsche follows the
old mule track along
which the German
philosopher com-
posed *Thus Spake
Zarathustra* in 1883
as he climbed from
his lodgings in Èze-
Bord-du-Mer up to
Èze Village (allow a
good hour for the climb).

Below: ancient
Olivier Millénaire olive
tree in Roquebrune.

The Basse Corniche then continues through **Monaco** *(see pp. 58–63)*. Take the Tunnel du Serrouville through Le Rocher to Port Hercule and follow signs for Menton, climbing up along boulevard des Moulins.

GRANDE CORNICHE

At the roundabout at the end of boule-vard d'Italie return to France, entering Roquebrune-Cap Martin on the D6098. Unless you are continuing on to **Menton** *(see pp. 64–9)*, fork left onto the D6007 and left towards Roque-brune-La Turbie on the D2564, or Grande Corniche, which was laid out under Napoleon and followed the route of the Roman Via Aurelia between Rome and Spain, also known in this section as the Via Julia Augusta.

Roquebrune Village

Turn off right to **Roquebrune Village** ❺, clinging to the hillside with its square castle sticking up behind the orange church. Park at the foot on place Birigliano, from where steps climb up to place des Deux-Frères, with a big olive tree framed by two dramatic lumps of rock (the two brothers of its name).

Lunch in **La Grotte**, see ⑪④, or smarter **Les Deux Frères**, see ⑪⑤, and admire the panorama of tower-block Monaco, before exploring the tangled alleyways of old Roquebrune, some of them (such as rue Montcollet) cut into the rock itself.

At the top, the **Château** (tel: 04 93 35 07 22; call for opening times; charge) was begun in 970 and enlarged by the Grimaldis of Monaco, who ruled Ro-quebrune until the town made its bid for independence in 1848, joining France in 1860. In 1910 Englishman Sir William Ingram began reconstruction, leaving the castle with a vaulted guardroom and rampart walk to the town in 1926.

Take rue de la Fontaine behind the **Église Ste-Margeurite** (daily 2–5pm) and go through the gateway, where the chemin de Gorbio leads up to the ceme-tery. Architect Le Corbusier, whose wooden *cabanon* on Cap Martin *(see feature, p.54)* is an icon of modern archi-tecture and who died when bathing off the Riviera in 1965, is among those buried here. In the other direction to the cemetery, a path leads down to the **Olivier Millénaire**, a gnarled olive tree which is over a thousand years old.

La Turbie

From Roquebrune, heading west, the Grande Corniche zigzags up between olive and pine trees and limestone out-crops for 8km (5 miles) to **La Turbie**, where the white marble columns of La Trophée des Alpes stand silhouetted against the skyline. The road leads through the edge of the village, where the **Café de la Fontaine**, see ⑪⑥, is a superb place for a meal.

Park on the square and go through one of the remaining medieval gateways and up plant-hung narrow streets to **La**

Trophée des Alpes ❻ (mid-May–mid-Sept Tue–Sun 9.30am–1pm and 2.30–6.30pm, mid-Sept–mid-May 10am–1.30pm and 2.30–5pm; charge), built around 6 BC in honour of Emperor Augustus who had subdued 45 Celto-Ligurian tribes. Subsequently sacked by barbarians and pillaged for building materials, La Trophée is still impressive, although the statue of the emperor that once stood on top has long since gone.

MOYENNE CORNICHE

Continue along the D2564, after about 2km (miles) turn left on the D45 and then, shortly after, join the D6007. This is the Moyenne Corniche, the most direct of the three roads, which was built in the 1920s. Park below Èze Village, which is accessible only on foot.

Èze Village

Perched on top of a rocky crag at 429m (1,407ft), **Èze Village** ❼ was a prized stronghold for the Celts, Romans, Saracens, Guelphs and Ghibellines, before becoming a possession of the House of Savoie until 1860. Èze was largely abandoned after the 1887 earthquake, but is now a little-too-well-restored tourist destination; the gift shops and tour groups that throng the narrow streets can be almost suffocating in summer.

Enter the village through La Posterne gateway and go up rue Principale to place du Planète, turning left to the Chapelle des Pénitents Blancs and passing **Le Troubadour**, see ⊕⑦, and the 18th-century **Église Notre Dame de l'Assomption**, which has a painted dome and lashings of fake marble. At the very top of the village, the **Jardin Exotique** (see www.eze-riviera.com for opening hours; charge), on the site of the castle razed by Louis XIV, is a feast of cactuses and succulents, and is dotted with strange terracotta statues.

Continue for about 10km (6 miles) along the D6007 to return to Nice.

Above from far left: Roquebrune; Église Ste-Margeurite.

Food and Drink 🍴

④ LA GROTTE
Place des Deux-Frères, Roquebrune Village; tel: 04 93 35 00 04; Thur–Tue L and D; €
A semi-troglodyte café and pizzeria with tables in the cave cut into the rock beneath the château or out on the square.

⑤ LES DEUX FRÈRES
Place des Deux-Frères, Roquebrune Village; tel: 04 93 28 99 00; summer Tue D, Wed–Sun L and D, winter Tue–Sat L and D, Sun D; €€
The old village school is now an attractive hotel and restaurant. Inviting, updated southern dishes might include artichoke salad or red mullet in a herb crust.

⑥ CAFÉ DE LA FONTAINE
4 avenue du Général de Gaulle, La Turbie; tel: 04 93 28 52 79; summer daily L and D, winter Tue–Sun L and D; €
Bruno Cirino of the acclaimed Hostellerie Jérôme took over the village café and turned it into a relaxed gourmet bistro, serving wonderful market-inspired regional cooking at remarkable prices. Reservations recommended.

⑦ LE TROUBADOUR
Rue du Brec, Èze Village; tel: 04 93 41 19 03; mid-Dec–mid-Nov Tue–Sun L and D; €€€
A long-established spot serving classic French cuisine and Provençal specialities in an old stone building in the centre of the village. Closed two weeks in March and early July.

MONACO

Tiny, densely populated Monaco is a curious monarchic anachronism in the midst of republican France, and packs in a fascinating mixture of architectural styles that go from royal palace to skyscraper city.

Telephone Code
Monaco has its own international dialling code; from outside the principality, dial 00 377 before the local number. In Monaco, just dial the eight-figure number for local calls, and remember to add 00 33 and omit the zero at the start of the ten-figure number to call a number in France.

DISTANCE 7.25km (4½ miles)
TIME A half day (allow a full day if visiting the palace and museums with time for lunch)
START Place d'Armes
END Casino de Monte-Carlo
POINTS TO NOTE

Monaco is divided into five areas, three of which are visited on this walk: Monaco-Ville or Le Rocher, La Condamine around the Port Hercule and Monte-Carlo around the Casino and its seaside extension Larvotto. The principality is tiny but hilly; a useful system of lifts and escalators connects its different levels. Only cars registered in Monaco or the Alpes-Maritimes can enter Monaco-Ville, so leave your car in one of the car parks in La Condamine. Monaco train station is underground; take the avenue Prince Pierre exit for place d'Armes; the square is also served by all six of Monaco's bus routes. All sights and museums close during the Monaco Grand Prix weekend (late May) when the town is transformed by grandstands and crash barriers.

Graham Greene described it as 'a sunny place for shady people', Katherine Mansfield called it 'Real Hell', yet there is something irresistibly absurd about this tiny mini state – the second smallest in Europe after the Vatican – which is famous for its Grand Prix, millionaire residents and tax haven status, and ruling monarchy. Tower blocks fight for space and sea views, dwarfing the remaining Belle Époque architecture and giving Monaco the air of a mini Hong Kong on the Mediterranean.

MARCHÉ DE LA CONDAMINE

Start on the arcaded **place d'Armes ❶**, which is about as close as Monaco gets to everyday life, with its morning outdoor fruit and vegetable stalls and the covered market at one end. Butchers, *charcutiers*, pasta stalls and a couple of small bars, all with photos of Prince Albert II, reflect the omnipresence of the royal family: although nominally a constitutional monarchy, power still resides with the prince.

MONACO-VILLE

Cross over to avenue de la Porte Neuve, which climbs the side of Le Rocher to Monaco-Ville, essentially a handful of streets lined with pastel-coloured houses, which lead to the palace. The street loops via avenue des Pins to place de la Visitation (you can also get here from place d'Armes by bus route nos 1 and 2). After admiring the chocolates in the window of the **Chocolaterie de Monaco** at the end of the square, fork right into rue Princesse Marie de Lorraine and its continuation rue Basse, a nonstop parade of souvenir shops, where you could be forgiven for thinking Monaco is a Ferrari franchise. For respite, pop into the surprisingly undervisited **Chapelle de la Miséricorde ❷** (daily 10am–6pm; free), with striped marble walls, white marble sculptures and a painted wood sculpture of the Dead Christ attributed to Monaco-born François Joseph Bosio (1768–1845).

Above from far left:
Port Hercule; a car registration indicates Monaco's status as a principality.

Above from left:
changing of the guard
at the Palais Princier;
stained-glass ele-
gance in the Café
de Paris; wealth is
everywhere to see.

Palais Princier

The street emerges on place du Palais, where cannons and neat pyramids of cannon balls are aligned in front of the **Palais Princier** ❸ (tel: +377-93 25 18 31; www.palais.mc; daily Apr 10.30am–6pm, May–Sept 9.30am–6.30pm, Oct 10am–5.30pm; charge), a storybook castle constructed around the fortress begun by Genoans in the 13th century. Each day, the changing of the guard takes place promptly at 11.55am, accompanied by much marching and drum beating. The worthwhile palace audio tour (complete with welcome from the Sovereign Prince) includes the frescoed

Galerie d'Hercule, one of the palace's Renaissance embellishments; the Galerie des Glaces, used to welcome guests during official receptions; and the Salle du Trône, where Prince Albert II was crowned in 2005.

Entered to the left of the State Apartments, the **Musée des Souvenirs Napoléoniens et Collection des Archives Historiques du Palais** (tel: +377-93 25 18 31; www.palais.mc; daily Apr 10.30am–6pm, May–Sept 9.30am–6.30pm, Oct 10am–5.30pm, Dec–Mar 10.30am–5pm; charge) is a much drier affair, although there is some interesting Napoleonic memorabilia that was amassed by Prince Louis II, a descendant of the emperor's adopted daughter Stéphanie de Beauharnais.

Cathédrale

Admire the views of Port Hercule and Port de Fontvieille from either side of the square, have a meal at **Castelroc**, see ⓧⓘ, or simply take rue Colonel Bellandro de Castro, passing the Conseil National (Monaco's parliament) and the Palais de Justice (law courts) to the 19th-century **Cathédrale** ❹ (daily 8am–6pm). It has a Romanesque-style façade and neo-Byzantine mosaic over the choir, and the side chapels contain saints' relics as well as an altarpiece by Louis Bréa. Around the apse are the simple slab-like royal tombs, the most recent being that of Prince Rainier II, alongside his beloved Princesse Grace.

Below: the cathedral.

*Musée Océanographique
et Aquarium*

From the cathedral, avenue St-Martin leads to the **Musée Océanographique et Aquarium** ❺ (tel: +377-93 25 18 31; www.oceano.mc; daily Apr–June and Sept 9.30am–7pm, July and Aug 9.30am–7.30pm, Oct–Mar 10am–6pm; charge), which hugs the cliffside. Upstairs is an old-fashioned museum largely devoted to the Arctic exploration trips of 'the scientist prince', Albert I (1848–1922), which is full of specimens preserved in formaldehyde, whale skeletons and mahogany cases of navigation charts. However, the chief draw is the enormously popular aquarium downstairs, where illuminated tanks, fed by water pumped in from the sea, include a shark pit and living coral reefs populated by brightly coloured Mediterranean and tropical species.

Exit and take the steps opposite back to place de la Visitation, where the 17th-century **Chapelle de la Visitation** ❻ (tel: 377-93 50 07 00; Tue–Sun 10am–4pm; charge) provides an appropriate Baroque setting for religious paintings by Rubens, Ribera and Zurbaran.

PORT HERCULE

Meander through the gardens beneath avenue de la Porte Neuve, which are dotted with sculptures by Arman *(see also p.46)* and others, and back across place d'Armes into rue Grimaldi. Turn right down pedestrianised rue Princesse Caroline to **Port Hercule** ❼, Monaco's natural deep-water harbour ever since the Phocaeans established their trading post, Monoikos. The broad terrace along boulevard Albert 1er is a prime spot for the Grand Prix but is also used for all sorts of events, from international showjumping in June to a funfair in August; below, the outdoor swimming pool becomes an ice rink in winter.

Turn right past **La Rascasse**, see ⑪②, to quai Antoine 1er, for exhibitions in the Salle des Exhibitions and American restaurant **Stars 'n' Bars**, see ⑪③.

Return along quai Antoine 1er and from the northeastern corner detour

What's On?
Try the useful official website www.monte-carlo.mc for information on most things going on in the principality.

Food and Drink 🍴

① CASTELROC
Place du Palais; tel: +377-93 30 36 68; www.restaurant-castelroc.com; Mon and Sun L only, Tue–Fri L and D; €€
This institution, with a cheerful, frescoed dining room and elegant conservatory overlooking the palace, is the place to try Monaco's Italianate specialities, such as *stocafi* (stockfish).

② LA RASCASSE
1 quai Antoine 1er; tel: +377-93 25 56 90; www.larascasse.mc; Mon–Fri L and D, Sat and Sun D only; €€
A two-storey restaurant and club that serves modish fish dishes at lunch and hosts live rock bands at night, with a grandstand view of the famous Rascasse bend.

③ STARS 'N' BARS
6 quai Antoine 1er; tel: +377-97 97 95 95; www.starsnbars.com; June–Sept daily L and D, Oct–May Tue–Sun; €€
Burgers and Tex-Mex are the name of the game at this hugely popular American restaurant, which has racing cars hanging from the ceiling and a huge terrace overlooking Port Hercule. There is a friendly welcome for all, from small children to racing drivers and pop stars. Food is served all day.

Jardin Exotique

This garden (62 boulevard du Jardin Exotique; www.jardin-exotique.mc; daily, summer 9am–7pm, winter until 6pm or dusk; charge), located on the western route out of town, is a fantasy land of cactuses and succulents. The entrance fee includes guided visits of the stalactite-filled Grotto de l'Observatoire and the Musée d'Anthropologie Préhistorique.

left up to **Église Ste-Dévote** (daily 8.30am–6pm), dedicated to the principality's patron saint, martyred Corsican virgin Saint Devota, who is said to have drifted ashore here in the 4th century. Although reconstructed in the 19th century and hemmed in by flyovers, the church has a strong symbolic importance for Monégasques, who burn a boat on the parvis every 26 January on the eve of the saint's feast.

Return to the port, following **quai des États-Unis**, where ogling the swanky yachts is a favourite pastime, to the new counter-jetty, part of the port's recent expansion. Now take the footpath that winds round the huge 1970s Complex des Spélugues, a series of overlapping hexagons, containing hotel, apartments and the Auditorium Rainier III congress centre, which juts out on concrete stilts into the water.

MONTE-CARLO

You emerge on avenue Princesse Grace, where the pretty **Jardin Japonais** (daily 9am–sunset; free) provides an oasis of oriental calm, with streams traversed by stepping stones and wooden bridges, Shinto shrines, raked gravel and trees trimmed into sculptural forms. Behind it is the polygonal glass and copper **Grimaldi Forum** (www.grimaldiforum.com), a busy congress, concert and exhibition centre overlooking the sea. It is worth going inside to check out the big summer art show or for a drink or meal at trendy **Karé(ment)**, see ⑪④.

Nouveau Musée National Poupées et Automates

Located in exotic gardens across the street, the **Nouveau Musée National Poupées et Automates** (tel: +377-93 30 91 26; www.nmnm.mc; daily 10am–6.30pm; charge), which is housed in the peaches-and-cream Villa Stauber, could hardly be a greater contrast. The doll-sized state's national museum focuses on elegantly attired porcelain dolls, along with all the miniature dinner services, rosewood furniture and copper jelly

---

Birth of Monte-Carlo

Monaco owes its transformation from obscure olive-growing hill town to gambling capital to the Grimaldis' loss of Menton and Roquebrune in the 1860s. In search of a new source of revenue, Prince Charles III had the bright idea of opening a casino on the Spelugues hill, creating a whole new district that he modestly named after himself. After an unenthusiastic start, the prince awarded the concession to run it to businessman François Blanc, founder of the Société des Bains de Monaco (SBM). In 1864 Blanc built the Hôtel de Paris to accommodate the principality's new visitors, and in 1878 his widow Marie called in architect Charles Garnier, who had recently designed the Paris Opéra, to tack a lavish opera house onto the back of the casino to encourage gamblers to stay in town a little longer. The SBM, now majority owned by the State of Monaco, still owns most of Monte-Carlo's finest hotels, restaurants, casinos, spa, sporting facilities and nightclubs, and certain old-fashioned principles still apply: no Monégasque citizens or clergymen are allowed into the gaming rooms.

Above from far left:
Casino de Monte-
Carlo; Jardin Exotique.

moulds suited to their station. The highlight of the museum is the fragile vintage automatons, which are set in motion several times a day.

To the east along avenue Princesse Grace is the **Plage du Larvotto**, Monaco's man-made beach, but to continue this walk take the lift next to the museum up to boulevard des Moulins. Turn left (west) past elegant antiques dealers and clothes shops.

Place du Casino

Just after the **Tourist Office** *(see p.105)*, the manicured fountains and herbaceous borders of the **Jardins Boulengrin** provide a fine vista down to **place du Casino**, the ensemble that encapsulates the Monte-Carlo myth. To the right, Rolls-Royces and Ferraris line up outside the **Hôtel de Paris**, first and still grandest of Monte-Carlo's grand hotels. On the corner, Cartier heralds the jewellers and couture boutiques that lead up avenue des Beaux-Arts to the palatial **Hôtel Hermitage**.

On the opposite side of the place du Casino, the terrace of the **Café de Paris**, see ⑤, is perfect for observing the comings and goings on the square; within, its slot machines are busy from early morning and a notice at the entrance to the brasserie tells you to check your fur coat into the cloakroom. For a cheaper pit stop, take avenue des Spélugues for **Le Tip Top**, see ⑥, where photos of important customers hang behind the bar.

Finish your walk at the legendary **Casino de Monte-Carlo** ⑫ (tel: +377-98 06 21 21; www.casinomontecarlo.com; Mon–Fri 2pm–late, Sat–Sun noon–late; over 18s only, ID required). Even if you are not a gambler, the ornate confection still has an aura of glamour. Inside, roulette and black jack are played against a backdrop of allegorical paintings and chandeliers, and across the foyer the **Salle Garnier** opera house, designed by Charles Garnier *(see feature, left)*, has been painstakingly restored right down to the five different shades of gold leaf.

Food and Drink

④ KARÉ(MENT)
Grimaldi Forum, 10 avenue Princesse Grace; tel: +377-99 99 20 20; www.karement.com; daily L and D; €€
The smart neo-Baroque bar and restaurant is absolutely the place to be, whether for breakfast on the terrace overlooking the sea, Provençal, Japanese and Chinese food at lunch, or cocktails and DJs at night.

⑤ CAFÉ DE PARIS
Place du Casino; tel: +377-98 06 76 23; www.montecarlo resort.com; daily L and D; €€€
A faithful recreation of the original Belle Époque bar and brasserie, next to the casino. There's great people-watching on the pavement terrace, plus a restaurant with 1900s decor and its own casino with car-themed slot machines. The *crêpe suzette* was invented here. Serves all day.

⑥ LE TIP TOP
11 avenue des Spélugues; tel: +377-93 50 69 13; daily L and D; €
A jovial, old-fashioned restaurant and bar that surprisingly still exists in Monte-Carlo, feeding steak and matchstick chips, spaghetti and pizzas to local workers at lunch and to absolutely everyone (including Prince Albert) in the dead of night.

MENTON

Famed for its mild climate and exotic vegetation, the most Italian of the French Riviera towns is worth exploring for its labyrinthine Old Town, lush tropical gardens and vestiges of its past as an aristocratic winter resort.

Tasty Treats

Menton has several culinary specialities. As well as lemon-meringue tart, try *tarte mentonnaise* or *pichade*, with onions, tomatoes, anchovies, garlic and olives on a pastry base, and *fougasse mentonnaise*, a cake flavoured with orange blossom water, sugar and aniseed.

DISTANCE 3.25km (2 miles)
TIME A full day
START Jardin Biovès
END Jardin Botanique Exotique Val Rahmeh
POINTS TO NOTE
Begin in the morning when the market is in full swing. The Jardin Biovès is easily reached from Menton train station along avenue de la Gare. From Jardin Botanique Exotique Val Rahmeh return to the town centre along the seafront.

Food and Drink

① RESTAURANT-PIZZERIA DES ARTISTES

1080 Promenade du Soleil; tel: 04 93 35 58 50; Mon D, Tue–Sun L and D; €€
Popular with locals and tourists alike. The tables outside on the seafront promenade are the real draw here, but it also serves up competent brasserie fare, such as king prawns, mussels, duck fillet and summer salads.

② HÔTEL-RESTAURANT DES ARCADES

41 avenue Félix Faure; tel: 04 93 35 70 62; www.hotel lesarcades.com; daily B, L and D; €
This bar and restaurant set under the arcades leading up to the town hall is a relaxed place for a drink or inexpensive meal. The kitchen makes an effort with homely southern recipes such as sea bream cooked with black olives.

Set against a backdrop of mountains just before the Italian frontier, Menton became established in the 13th century on a rocky promontory on the old Roman road from Italy. From 1346, it was ruled by the Grimaldis of Monaco until 1848 when the town declared independence in protest against high taxes on lemons and olive oil, and then voted to become part of France in 1860. Soon it became a favourite destination of the British, Germans and Russians, thanks to Dr Henry Bennett who prescribed the health benefits of winters by the sea. Belle Époque villas, grand hotels, Anglican and Russian Orthodox churches were built and green-fingered visitors, many of them English, made the most of the exceptional climate (Menton claims to have 316 sunny days a year) to introduce tropical plants.

MODERN MENTON

Jardin Biovès

Start your walk down the palm- and orange-tree lined **Jardin Biovès** . Laid out as an elegant promenade over the River Cenci at the end of the 19th century, for two weeks each February it becomes the focus of Menton's Fête du Citron *(see p.23)*, when its lawns are filled with giant sculptures made out of oranges and lemons. About halfway down, on avenue Boyer, the fanciful **Palais de l'Europe ②**, once the grand casino, is now home to the **Tourist Office** *(see p.105)*, municipal library and a contemporary art gallery.

The **Casino ③**, fronting the sea at the southern end of the gardens, was built in the 1930s with a wavelike Art Deco silhouette. As if in disapproval, the Anglican Church of St John's, an incongruous Victorian Gothic building, turns its back on the casino, although the gambling there is quietly genteel compared to the glamour of nearby Monaco.

Promenade du Soleil

Go round to the right of the casino to the **promenade du Soleil**, which borders the long pebble beach and is lined with an eclectic mix of Belle Époque villas, modern apartment blocks and hotels, and brasseries that do a hard sell with their pavement terraces (try **Restaurant-Pizzeria des Artistes**, see ⑪①, near the casino).

Follow the promenade eastwards, then turn left up rue Adhémar de Lantagnac, turning right at the roundabout into avenue Félix Faure. Here, you might want to pause for a drink or meal at the deep-red, arcaded **Hôtel-Restaurant des Arcades**, see ⑪②.

Salle des Mariages

From the restaurant, cross the small garden square to the Hôtel de Ville to visit the **Salle des Mariages ④** (tel: 04 92 10 50 00; Mon–Fri 8.30am–12.30pm, 2–5pm; charge), which was

Collection Séverin Wunderman

Menton's Cocteau connection was recently enhanced by a major donation from art collector Séverin Wunderman of 1,440 works spanning Cocteau's career, along with works by Modigliani, De Chirico, Foujita, Magritte and Man Ray. An exciting new museum designed by Rudy Ricciotti, resembling a white octopus, is due to open in spring 2011.

Below: Vieux Menton.

decorated by the artist, poet and filmmaker Jean Cocteau in the 1950s. Ring ahead to check, as it is sometimes booked up by tour groups and is still used for ceremonies.

After the town hall's classical exterior, the room comes as a vibrant, jazzy surprise from the whimsical murals to the Spanish chairs, mock panther carpet and lamps shaped like prickly pears. For the murals, Cocteau's aim was to 'create a theatrical setting… to offset the officialdom of a civil ceremony', and his inspiration was the Riviera style at the turn of the 20th century, 'a mood redolent of Art Nouveau villas decorated with swirling seaweed, irises and flowing hair'. On the wall above the official's desk, Cocteau depicts the engaged couple – she wears a Mentonnais straw hat, he's in a fisherman's cap – trying to read the future in each other's eyes.

Halles Municipales

Return to avenue Félix Faure, which soon runs into the busy pedestrianised rue St-Michel. On the right at the end of place Clemenceau is the **Halles Municipales** ❺, a covered market, adorned with a glazed ceramic frieze of comical sculpted faces, which offers a profusion of local produce every morning. At the far end, turn left through **place aux Herbes**, an attractive arcaded square of chestnut trees, back to rue St-Michel.

Rue St-Michel

Along with a lot of tourist tack, you can sample real Menton lemon juice and beer brewed in the nearby village of Castillon at **Mare Nostrum** (near the junction with rue Pièta) and delicious ice creams from **Tutti Frutti** (no. 24). Next door, the elegant **Hôtel d'Adhémar de Lantagnac** ❻ (tel: 04 92 10 97 10; Tue–Sat 10am–12.30pm, 1.30–5.30pm), belonging to the Service de Patrimoine, has exhibitions on Menton's architectural heritage.

Now cross place du Cap, just to the east, where **L'Ulivo**, see ⑪③, and other restaurant terraces cluster around an olive tree, and descend tiny rue Capierra and rue du Jonquiers to the seafront.

Bastion Musée Jean Cocteau

Cross the street to the **Vieux Port**, where the 17th-century bastion on the western jetty houses the **Bastion Musée Jean Cocteau** ❼ (tel: 04 93 57 72 30; Wed–Mon 10am–noon, 2–6pm; charge). The tiny museum is quickly viewed but has the charm of a scenography overseen by the artist himself, although he died shortly before it opened in 1966. Cocteau adapted his graphic style to the pebble mosaics or *calades* character-istic of the town – a young couple and a schematised face gaze out from either side of the entrance and *La Salamandre* covers the floor down-stairs. In the upstairs guards' room, still with its brick oven, changing dis-plays of drawings, lithographs and archive photos focus on Cocteau's Mediterranean period, along with engaging pottery jars influenced by Greek and Etruscan designs. A second Cocteau museum is currently being built on the esplanade opposite Les Halles *(see margin, left)*.

Across the street from the Bastion Musée Jean Cocteau, **Le Nautic**, see ⑪④, is another possible lunch spot.

VIEUX MENTON

Now follow **quai Bonaparte** north. Amid pavement restaurants, go through a discreet colonnade to the Rampes St-Michel, a steep double flight of steps with pebble *calades* climbing up to the church. Halfway up, turn left then right onto **rue Longue**. This was once Menton's main thoroughfare; Prince Honoré II of Monaco had a palace here in the early 17th century. The street still feels like an Italian hill village, with its tall orange houses, some of them still occupied by craftsmen, and countless dark stairways and alleys leading off on either side.

Consider stopping at no. 66, where **A Braïjade Méridiounale**, see ⑪⑤, is an atmospheric place for trying Mentonnais specialities.

Food and Drink

③ RESTAURANT L'ULIVO

21 place du Cap; tel: 04 93 35 45 65; www.restaurant-ulivo.com; Tue–Sat L and D, Sun L; €€

Occupying a listed building on a pretty square, this restaurant offers well-prepared Sardinian specialities, including vegetable antipasti, roast suckling pig, plump stuffed pasta, octopus and mountain ham and liqueurs made from myrtle.

④ LE NAUTIC

27 quai de Monléon; tel: 04 93 35 78 74; daily L and D; €€

A good fish restaurant with friendly Italian owners, located opposite the Bastion Musée Cocteau. Try generous por-tions of fried squid, John Dory with courgettes or sea bass cooked in a salt crust, and the strawberry sabayon for dessert.

⑤ A BRAÏJADE MÉRIDIOUNALE

66 rue Longue; tel: 04 93 35 65 65; www.abraijade.com; July–Aug daily D, Sept–June Thur–Tue L and D; €

Authentic regional cooking is served in an ancient beamed dining room hidden in the Old Town. Specialities include vegetable fritters, flame-grilled skewered meats and fish, *ravioles au pistou*, and *bagna caouda* or *anchoïade*.

Basilique St–Michel Archange

At **Porte St-Julien**, one of the original town gateways, double back along rue Mattoni until a fanciful archway brings you out at the **Basilique St-Michel Archange** ❽ (tel: 04 92 10 97 10; July–Aug daily 3–5.15pm, Sept–June 10am–noon and 3–5.15pm; free), a highlight of the region's Baroque architecture. Its campanile dominates Menton's skyline, and the square in front, paved with a grey-and-white pebble *calade* of the Grimaldi coat of arms, is the setting for Menton's prestigious chamber music festival each August *(see p.22)*. The church was begun in 1640, although its sculpted pink-and-ochre façade was rebuilt in 1819. The interior, restored after the 1887 earthquake, is surprisingly large with an arcaded triple nave, crystal chandeliers, elaborate side chapels, and a flamboyantly painted ceiling depicting St Michael slaying the dragon.

Chapelle des Pénitents Blancs

In the adjacent square stands the ornate **Chapelle des Pénitents Blancs** ❾, or Chapelle de l'Immaculée Conception, which was built in 1687 for a lay confraternity who sought to return to a simpler faith. If you are lucky enough to be here on a Wednesday afternoon (3–5pm if volunteers are present; free) or during the music festival, when it is used for early evening concerts by up-and-coming young musicians, you can visit the beautifully restored interior. Almost life-size stone statues of saints in niches ring the walls and a Baroque ceiling represents Heaven as a Mediterranean paradise. The chapel looks particularly astonishing during certain religious festivals when the walls around the statues, columns and pulpit are entirely covered in red satin hangings.

Cimetière du Vieux-Château

Go round the right-hand side of the chapel and take the steep montée du Souvenir. A gateway on the right leads into the **Cimetière du Vieux-Château** ❿ (May–Sept daily 7am–8pm, Oct–Apr daily 7am–6pm; free), built on the site of the medieval castle, which was demolished in 1807 after being appropriated as state property following the French Revolution. The slightly dilapidated lower tiers mainly contain British, German and Russian tombs, crowded with memorials to retired surgeons and major generals and the wives and daughters of good families. Overlooking the sea, the grave of the Reverend William Webb Ellis is full of tributes to the man 'who with a fine disregard for the rules of football first took the ball in his arms and ran with it, thus originating the distinctive feature of the rugby game'. A little further along is an elaborate Russian chapel complete with onion dome and coloured tiles, which commemorates a Russian prince.

GARAVAN

Leave the cemetery to the north on place du Cimetière, where a viewing terrace brings you out onto **boulevard de Garavan**, laid out in 1883 when the prosperous suburb of Garavan was being built with lavish villas and luxuriant gardens. The roadside is draped with bougainvillea, mimosa, succulents, cypresses and other exotic trees, some of which are labelled at pavement level.

Jardin Botanique Exotique Val Rahmeh

Several footpaths lead down to the Garavan seafront. After 36bis Villa Aurélia, take the unkempt sentier de la Villa Noël down between terraced gardens to the **Jardin Botanique Exotique Val Rahmeh ❶** (tel: 04 93 35 86 72; Oct–Mar Wed–Mon 10am–12.30pm and 2–5pm, Apr–Sept 10am–12.30pm and 3–6pm; charge); turn left on avenue St-Jacques for the entrance.

This fascinating botanical garden, now run by the Muséum National d'Histoire Naturel in Paris, was created in the 1920s by retired governor of Malta, Lord Percy Radcliffe, around a villa and lily pond. In the 1950s, the next owner introduced numerous plants from Asia, Africa and the Americas, notably the pretty but poisonous daturas that earned her the nickname 'La Dame aux Daturas'.

A winding trail leads round between magical and medicinal plants, dry and wet environments, towering palms, dank tropical ferns, forests of bamboo and exotic cocoa, avocado, banana, guava and citrus fruits, tea bushes and spice trees, and even the mythic Sophoro Toromiro tree, which is now extinct on its native Easter Island.

Below: Menton's Fête du Citron.

Tropical Gardens

East of Val Rahmeh are four more remarkable gardens, which can be visited by appointment with the Maison du Patrimoine (tel: 04 92 10 33 66): poetic Jardin des Colombières (created in 1919–27) was inspired by Greek and Roman mythology, mixing Mediterranean vegetation and antique sculpture; Fontana Rosa (dating from the 1920s) features tiled pergolas and pools; palm-filled gardens at Villa Maria Serena (built in the 1880s and designed by Charles Garnier); and the Clos du Peyronnet, created by the Waterfield family in 1915, around steps of water.

On the other side of town, the romantic gardens of the Serre de la Madone (74 route de Gorbio; tel: 04 93 57 73 90; Tue–Sun 10am–5pm (summer until 6pm); charge) were designed in the 1920s by Lawrence Johnston, creator of the garden at Hidcote Manor in England, with geometric pools, terraces and rare flora from around the globe.

VENCE

Still ringed by ramparts and a curving wall of buildings punctuated by gateways, the historic centre of Vence forms an attractive labyrinth, where traces of the Roman town of Ventium can still be seen amid the medieval lanes.

DISTANCE 1km (¾ mile)
TIME A half day
START Place du Grand Jardin
END Château de Villeneuve – Fondation Emile Hugues
POINTS TO NOTE

From Nice get to Vence via Cagnes-sur-Mer (either taking the D6007 or the *autoroute* A8) then take the D36 and park in the car park under Place du Grand Jardin; you can also take a bus (nos 400 or 94) from Nice via Cagnes-sur-Mer or a taxi from Cagnes-sur-Mer.

Food and Drink 🍽

① **LE TROQUET**

13 place du Grand Jardin; tel: 04 93 58 64 31; Mon–Sat L and D; €
A relaxed place to pause for a coffee, salad, bruschetta or good-value daily specials such as grilled prawns or roast lamb.

Old Vence's two main sights – the old cathedral and former château of the lords of Villeneuve – point to the power struggle between bishops and nobility that long dominated the town. With the eruption of the French Revolution in 1789, Bishop Pisani was forced to flee the country and the see was never restored. Vence drifted into a steady decline so that by the beginning of the 20th century, it was half deserted, with many houses in ruins. After World War I, writers and artists including André Gide, D.H. Lawrence, Raoul Dufy, Marc Chagall and Chaim Soutine were drawn to the town. Today, tourism and sunbelt industries have transformed Vence into a bustling centre of more than 17,000 people, with a surprisingly well-preserved walled and oval Old Town defying the urban sprawl.

Start your walk at **place du Grand-Jardin ❶**, situated on the edge of the historic centre and home to the **farmers' market** (Tue–Sun am), a **flea market** on Wednesdays, Les Nuits du Sud summer world music festival *(see p.22)*, the **Tourist Office** *(see p.105)*, and several bistros and cafés, including **Le Troquet**, see ⑪①.

PORTE DU PEYRA

From the northeastern corner of the square, cross avenue Henri Isnard and go through the **Porte du Peyra ❷**, an arched gateway through the city wall, adjoining a fortified 12th-century tower. A tablet proclaims the virtues of the **Source de la Foux**, a spring bringing delicious fresh calcium-rich water from the mountain to the drinking fountain beneath the adjacent 19th-century urn-shaped fountain. Behind on the **place du Peyra**, probable forum of the Roman city of Ventium, ancient chestnut trees shade the café and restaurant terraces, and the **Poterie du Peyra** provides a tasteful selection of Provençal pottery, table linen and kitchenwares.

Cross the square and turn right into narrow **rue du Marché**, where the former ground-floor stables and kitchens now contain a colourful array of excellent food shops; admire cheeses and wines at **Poivre d'Ane**, or pick up supplies for a picnic. Turn left up ruelle de la Mairie to place Clemenceau, home to the **Hôtel de Ville** (town hall), inaugurated in 1911 on the site of the former bishop's palace.

CATHÉDRALE

To its right is the **Cathédrale ❸**, built between the 12th and 15th centuries on the site of an earlier Merovingian church which was in turn built on top of a Roman temple dedicated to Mars. From 374 until the French Revolution, Vence was a bishopric and had a tradition of powerful clerics: the bishops Véran (5th century) and Lambert (12th century) were both declared saints, while Farnese (16th century) declined the Vence bishop's crosier, going instead to the Holy See to become Pope Paul III. He proved to be

Above: Vence.

St-Paul-de-Vence

Just 4km (2½ miles) from Vence, St-Paul-de-Vence is another art-lover's must for the beautifully displayed works by Braque, Miro, Léger, Chagall and other modern artists at the Fondation Maeght (tel: 04 93 32 81 63; www.fondation-maeght.com). To appreciate picturesque St-Paul itself, visit out of season or in the early evening when the coach tours have gone and you have the rampart views and narrow streets to yourself.

Left: the cathedral's ornate entrance.

quite generous to Vence, however, and donated several reliquaries.

The unusual side entrance has painted cherubs over the doorway and Roman tablets inserted into the pilasters on either side of the door. The one on the left is inscribed from Ventium to Godium II 239 AD and on the right to the Emperor Elagabad in 220.

Inside is a triple-naved Romanesque structure with numerous fragments of Carolingian carving from the earlier church incorporated into the walls and columns. Set into an elaborate sculpted frame behind the font is a delicate mosaic designed by Chagall, depicting the baby Moses in his cradle in the bulrushes against a sparkling sun. Also worth admiring are the 15th-century oak and pear-wood choir stalls carved by Jacques Bellot of Grasse, alive with animals, plants and sometimes irreverent details of clerical life.

ALONG THE MOAT

Leave the cathedral and double back across the square into rue Alsace Lorraine to take the **Porte du Pontis** ❹, which is a vaulted passage that emerges onto avenue Marcelin Maurel. This was once the moat that divided the walled town from the outer *faubourgs* (districts).

Turn left and follow what is now a busy shopping street until place Antony Mars, and return to the old city through the 13th-century **Porte du Signadour** ❺ (Provençal for lookout post) into rue de l'Hôtel de Ville.

Turn right down **rue St-Lambert**, a characterful medieval street, taking a look on the way at the archway, on the right with a Roman stele inserted into the wall, which leads into evocatively named place de l'Enfer (Hell).

Matisse's Chapel

On the outskirts of Vence towards St-Jeannet, the Chapelle du Rosaire (468 avenue Henri Matisse; tel: 04 93 58 03 26; Mon, Wed and Sat 2–5.30pm, Tue and Thur 10–11.30am and 2–5.30pm; charge) is the spiritual masterpiece of Henri Matisse (1869–1954). It was designed between 1947–51 in gratitude to the young Dominican nun Sister Jacques-Marie, who had nursed and sat for him when he was living in Vence in Villa la Rêve during World War II. The elderly artist conceived everything from the building itself, with its blue-and- white glazed pantiles and simple lancet windows, to the gilded crucifix on the altar. The calm interior is a wonderful mix of Matisse's mastery of line, as seen in *St Dominic, the Virgin and Child* and the *Stations of the Cross* drawn in black on white tiles, and of colourful stained glass, the reflections of which send dapples of yellow and green across the walls. Too ill to attend the opening ceremony, Matisse none-theless sent along a text: 'This work took four years of assiduous work and is the summary of all my active life. I consider it, des-pite all its imperfections, as my masterpiece.'

AROUND PLACE GODEAU

At the end of rue St-Lambert, turn left into **place Godeau ❻**, the pleasant tree-lined square behind the cathedral, named after 17th-century poet bishop Antoine Godeau, who was a founder member of the Académie Française. In the centre is a granite Roman column.

To the right of the narrow Gothic doorway at no. 5, take rue des Portiques, which overlies part of the Roman road between Cimiez and Castellane, and turn left at the end into rue St-Véran, one of the main thoroughfares through the town. Explore the series of narrow, stepped streets such as impasse du Cimetière Vieux, rue Ste-Elisabeth, rue Pisani and rue Ste-Luce, which lead off it to **boulevard Paul André ❼**, where the once imposing ramparts have been cut down to provide beautiful views of Les Baous mountains.

CHÂTEAU DE VILLENEUVE

Take rue Pisani into **rue de l'Evêché**, full of craft galleries and artists' studios, as well as bistro **La Litote**, see ⓘ②.

Head west back to place du Peyra. On the edge of the square is the rear entrance of the **Auberge des Seigneurs**, see ⓘ③, a historic inn that is still a fine place to stay or eat. Also here is the **Château de Villeneuve – Fondation Emile Hugues ❽** (tel: 04 93 58

15 78; July–Sept Tue–Sun 10am–6pm, Oct–June Tue–Sun 10am–12.30pm and 2–6pm; charge), the 17th-century mansion of the lords of Villeneuve, which can be entered through the bookshop beside Porte du Peyra or from place du Frêne.

Inside, leading off a grandiose balustraded staircase, are well-restored, light-filled rooms – some of them still with carved wooden fireplaces and stucco doorways and chimneypieces – as well as a tiny square *cabinet* (tiny room) with a frescoed ceiling, which are used for interesting temporary exhibitions of modern and contemporary art.

Leave the Château on place du Frêne, where the ash tree in the centre is supposed to have been planted in 1538 in honour of the visit by François 1er and Pope Paul III.

Food and Drink

② LA LITOTE

5 rue de l'Evêché; tel: 04 93 24 27 82; www.lalitote.com; Tue–Sat L and D; Sun L; €€
This friendly bistro brings an imaginative whiff of modernity to southern cuisine. Try dishes like foie gras crème brûlée, beef in red wine sauce or a trio of red mullet, sea bream and scallops with quinoa risotto. Live jazz on Thursday nights.

③ AUBERGE DES SEIGNEURS

Place du Frêne; tel: 04 93 58 04 24; May–Oct Tue–Sat L and D; €€
Spanning a wing of the château between place du Frêne and place du Peyra, this venerable inn has welcomed centuries of illustrious and ordinary travellers, serving classic Provençal dishes in a dining room with a beautiful fireplace. There are also six good-sized bedrooms furnished with old furniture and pretty rugs.

ANTIBES

Historic Antibes is a year-round destination with its busy yacht harbour, one of the best food markets on the Riviera, and a fascinating collection of works by Picasso in the beautifully restored castle.

DISTANCE 2.25km (1½ miles)	
TIME A half day	
START/END Port Vauban	
POINTS TO NOTE	

From the station, the port is easily reached along avenue de la Libération and avenue de Verdun. If arriving by car, park along the port and avoid driving in Vieil Antibes itself, which is semi-pedestrianised and has a complicated one-way system.

Le Fort Carré
Crowning a promontory north of the port, the Fort Carré (avenue du 11 novembre, tel: 06 14 89 17 45; Tue–Sun 10am–4pm (mid-June–mid-Sept to 5.30pm), guided tours every 30 mins; charge) is a masterpiece of military engineering. Begun by Henri II in the 16th century and improved by Vauban in the 17th, it has four pointed bastions around a circular central keep. No longer used by the military, it had a cameo role in the 1983 James Bond movie *Never Say Never Again* and the rampart walk offers superb views.

Right: narrow street in the Old Town.

Layers of history are piled up in fortified old Antibes as its medieval buildings sit above those of its Ancient Greek and Roman predecessors. Founded in the 5th century BC by Phocaean Greeks from Marseille who named it Antipolis, Antibes was a keystone in French naval strategy against the Comté of Nice. Sacked twice by Emperor Charles V in the 16th century, kings Henri II and Henri III added new fortifications; in 1680 Louis XIV brought in his brilliant military engineer Vauban to give it the impressive set of star-shaped ramparts and bastions that still line the shore. Unlike the holiday hedonism of adjacent Juan-les-Pins and the exclusive Cap d'Antibes *(see p.78)*, Antibes itself has a lived-in, all-year appeal, with its cobbled shopping streets, lively cafés and a big expat community serving the yachting fraternity.

PORT VAUBAN

Now the largest yacht marina in Europe with berths for over 2,000 boats, spawning a whole industry of shipbrokers, outfitters and crews, **Port Vauban ❶** gave Antibes its strategic importance, especially when Antibes was a stronghold of the French crown against Genoese-ruled Nice just up the coast. On the southeastern corner of the Vieux Port, a small archway leads through the harbour wall to the **Plage de la Gravette**, a small sandy beach.

Porte Marine

Go through the **Porte Marine ②**, long the sole entrance to the town from the port, through La Courtine defensive wall, which still has cannon barrels sticking out to sea, into rue Aubernon. On your left, the rampe des Saleurs, recalling the fish salting activity that used to take place here, brings you out to the rampart walk along promenade Amiral de Grasse; note the plaque on the house where painter Nicolas de Staël lived in 1954–5.

VIEIL ANTIBES

A little further on, go through the arch on rue des Arceaux to enter the pretty maze of small streets and houses of Vieil Antibes. Turn left down rue St-Esprit to the forecourt of the **Église de l'Im-maculée Conception ③**. Its ochre and russet classical façade hides a much earlier structure, which even had the status of cathedral from the 5th century until 1236. The interior is surprisingly simple with no side chapels but plenty of gaudy gilded side altars and a Romanesque east end. The square Romanesque bell tower in front is a converted 12th-century 'Saracen' watchtower.

Musée Picasso

On leaving, take the steps to the side of the square up to the severe stone Château Grimaldi, now home to the **Musée Picasso ④** (tel: 04 92 90 54 20; mid-June–mid-Sept Tue–Sun 10am–6pm (July and Aug Wed and Fri until 8pm), mid-Sept–mid-June Tue–Sun 10am–noon and 2–6pm; charge). Built on the site of the Greek acropolis and Roman *castrum*, the castle was the bishop's palace before becoming a residence of the Grimaldi

Above from far left: fortified Antibes; plage de la Gravette.

Plage de Salis

Antibes' best public beach is just a 15-minute walk south of Vieil Antibes. Long, curving and sandy, it is very popular with families. Plage de la Garoupe, further around the Cap, has higher snob value but is largely taken up by private beach restaurants.

family from 1385 until 1608, when it and the port were sold to the French crown. It then successively served as residence of the king's governor, town hall, barracks, and then the city's first archaeological museum. In 1946, curator and archaeologist Romuald Dor de la Souchère proposed to let Picasso, who was living in Antibes with his new companion Françoise Gilot, use the large room on the second floor as a studio. Between September and November, Picasso worked here frenetically. Lack of materials after the war meant that he often used Ripolin household paint and unlikely supports like fibrocement and chipboard, even painting

some graphic faces directly onto the wall. Picasso left behind 23 paintings and 44 drawings, which form the focus of the recently enlarged and renovated museum.

The Collection

In the former studio are some of the main works Picasso created here, including his celebrated *Joie de Vivre* (The Joy of Life), a cheerful frieze of music-playing animals and dancing goats, a monochrome triptych *Satyre, Faune et Centaure*, the gutsy *Le Gobeur d'Oursins* (The Sea Urchin Eater) and a study for his sculpture *The Goat*, as well as engaging animal-shaped pottery jugs. Other rooms include two

Right: Église de l'Immaculée Conception.

Above from far left:
Musée Picasso;
Marché Provençal
and Absinthe Bar.

striking, highly simplified reclining nudes, still lifes with fish and sea urchins, clearly inspired by the local catch, and numerous drawings, varying from rigorous geometric studies to portraits of Françoise.

Picasso was not the only artist drawn to Antibes, and the museum visit starts on the ground floor with the gestural abstraction of Hans Hartung (1904–89) and the more minimalist style, often combined with gold leaf, of his companion Anna-Eva Bergman.

On the first floor are powerful works by Russian-born abstract artist Nicolas de Staël (1914–55), including *Le Grand Concert*, left unfinished at his death, and *Nude*, showing his use of thinner paint and return to figurative elements at the end of his life. There are also contemporary works by Tapiès, Picabia and Léger, among others; note that these paintings are not always on view during temporary exhibitions.

Before you leave, go out onto the terrace, where bronzes by Germaine Richier (1902–59) gaze out to sea from the ramparts alongside sculptures by Arman and Miro.

Marché Provençal

Return down the steps and turn left beside the town hall into broad cours Masséna, where the iron-framed covered market is home to the wonderful **Marché Provençal** ❺ (June–Aug daily 6am–1pm, Sept–May Tue–Sun 6am–1pm), a rather upmarket food market

full of tempting fruit and vegetables, goat's cheeses, *tapenades* and dried sausages; in summer, there's also an afternoon **craft market** (Thur–Sun).

The square is arcaded on one side, with small cafés and specialist food shops. Investigate the unusual **Absinthe Bar** (which is beneath olive oil specialist Balade en Provence), with its entrance round the corner on rue Sade, see ⑪①.

At the southern end of the square, take the small flight of steps through the Portail de l'Orme into rue de l'Orme – the two round towers you can see are a remnant of medieval wall, built over Roman foundations – and head back to the ramparts.

Food and Drink 🍴

① L'ABSINTHE BAR

25 cours Masséna; tel: 04 93 34 93 00; June–Aug daily 9am–midnight, Sept–May Tue–Sat 9am–midnight
Located beneath a shop selling olive oil and other Provençal delicacies is this atmospheric cellar bar – complete with bits of Roman masonry – dedicated to the green fairy or absinthe, the favourite drink of the Impressionists. Dozens of varieties of absinthe (minus the wormwood that made the 19th-century version poisonous) and pastis are on offer amid a 'museum' of absinthe fountains, advertising memorabilia and strange hats to try on.

② LE BASTION

1 avenue du Général Maizière; tel: 04 93 34 59 86; www.restaurant-bastion.com; July–Aug Sun–Fri L and D, Sat D, mid-Sept–mid-June Sun and Tue–Fri L and D, Sat D; €€
This trendy, designer restaurant set into the ramparts has tables inside with views of the open kitchen and outside with views of the sea. The imaginative global menu runs from France to Japan and Spain to Guadeloupe.

Cap d'Antibes

Jutting into the sea between Antibes and Juan-les-Pins, wooded Cap d'Antibes is a millionaire's paradise, home to the famous Hôtel du Cap and the palatial villas of Arab princes and Russian oligarchs. At its summit, the Phare de la Garoupe lighthouse is a pleasant walk from Port de Salis up the stony (bring good shoes) chemin du Calvaire to the Plateau de la Garoupe, where the Chapelle de la Garoupe (daily 10am–noon and 2.30–5pm) has been a site of pilgrimage for centuries.

As with many of the Riviera's exclusive headlands, however, the nearest you are likely to get to its luxury residences is their imposing gateways. One exception is Villa Eilenroc (tel: 04 93 67 74 33; Sept–June house Wed 9am–noon and 1.30–5pm, gardens Tue–Wed and Sat 9.30am–5pm), which was designed by Charles Garnier of Paris and Monte-Carlo opera houses fame. You can reach it via the Sentier Tir-Poil coastal footpath, which winds round tiny unspoilt bays and rocky promontories from Plage de la Garoupe (allow about an hour; *pictured*). The villa's rose-, eucalyptus- and palm-tree filled gardens provide the stage for the Musiques au Coeur festival in July. An alternative is a cruise in the Visio Bulle (Apr–Sept from Ponton Courbet, Juan-les-Pins; tel: 04 93 67 02 11; www.visiobulle.com), which allows you to spy on fish through its glass hull and the reclusive residents of Millionaires' Bay from the deck.

MUSÉE D'ARCHÉOLOGIE

Continue along promenade Amiral de Grasse, with views of Cap d'Antibes, to **Le Bastion** restaurant, see ⑪② *(p.77)*, and the 1698 Bastion St-André, the southern extremity of Vauban's defences, which contains the **Musée d'Archéologie** ❻ (mid-June–mid-Sept Tue–Sun 10am–noon and 2–6pm (July and Aug Wed and Fri until 8pm), mid-Sept–mid-June Tue–Sun 10am–1pm and 2–5pm; charge). Finds from archaeological digs and underwater shipwrecks, displayed in two long barrel-vaulted gunpowder rooms, illustrate the past importance of Antibes; among them are the *Galet d'Antibes* (Antibes Pebble), a large oval stone with curious inscriptions dating from the 5th century BC, pots testifying to trade with Greece and Etruria, amphorae and ancient anchors, Roman stelae, funerary urns and a mosaic from a Roman villa.

QUARTIER DU SAFRANIER

From the museum, follow rue du Haut-Castelet left to place Nikos Kazantzaki, which honours the Greek author of *Zorba the Greek* who wrote many of his plays and novels in Antibes. Here, orange and yellow signs announce that you are entering the **Commune Libre du Safranier**, an arty, boho district, which proudly proclaimed independence in the 1960s and still elects its own mayor and councillors.

Above: Port Vauban.

Take rue du Bas-Castelet, lined with picturesque small houses amid a profusion of creepers and window boxes, and turn right into rue des Pêcheurs and rue du Safranier to arrive in place du Safranier, where **La Taverne du Safranier**, see ⑪③, is popular for lunch.

Return to rue du Bas-Castelet, turning left at the end into rue de la Pompe, where, at no. 2, **Boulangerie Veziano** (Wed–Sun 6am–1pm and 4.30–7.30pm) produces superb *tourte de blettes (see p.15)* – both sweet and savoury versions. Now follow rue des Bains into rue James Close; the latter is full of interesting restaurants, art galleries and craft and jewellery shops.

PLACE NATIONALE

At rue de la République, Vieil Antibes' main shopping street, turn left for a shellfish feast at **L'Oursin**, see ⑪④, or right to reach **place Nationale**. The square is thought to be on the site of the Roman forum, busy with café terraces under the plane trees in summer and the Christmas market in winter. The column in the middle was a present to royalist Antibes from Louis XVIII in gratitude for keeping Napoleon out after his escape from Elba.

You may want to pop into the **Musée Peynet et du Dessin Humoristique** ❼ (tel: 04 92 90 54 30; mid-June–mid-Sept Tue–Sun 10am–6pm (July and Aug Wed and Fri until 8pm), mid-Sept–mid-June Tue–Sun 10am–noon and 2–6pm; charge). The collection centres on drawings by popular cartoonist Raymond Peynet, best known for his whimsical *Les Amoureux de Peynet* (Peynet's Lovers), but also features the work of other caricaturists.

TOWARDS PORT VAUBAN

On the opposite side of the square, take rue Thuret and turn right into boulevard d'Aiguillon, a broad street running along the inside of La Courtine defensive wall, which is packed with restaurants and loud expat pubs, such as **The Hop Store** and **The Colonial Pub**, frequented by Antibes' large British yachting set. Set into the casement wall, the **Galerie des Bains Douches** puts on exhibitions in the former municipal bathhouse. Go past the fountain at the end of the street to return to Porte Marine and the port.

Food and Drink

③ LA TAVERNE DU SAFRANIER

1 place du Safranier; tel: 04 93 34 80 50; July and Aug Mon and Tue D, Wed–Sun L and D, Sept, Oct and Mar–June Tue–Sat L and D, Sun L; €€
This convivial bistro with tables on a square in the Quartier du Safranier is a stalwart of the Commune and very popular with arty locals. Well-prepared regional dishes include *aioli*, grilled red pepper salad, marinated sardines, ravioli, the fresh fish of the day and a gigantic lemon meringue tart.

④ L'OURSIN

16 rue de la République; tel: 04 93 34 13 46; daily L and D; €€
Big platters of shellfish are the speciality at this long-established fish restaurant, which has a nautically themed interior as well as tables outside on the square.

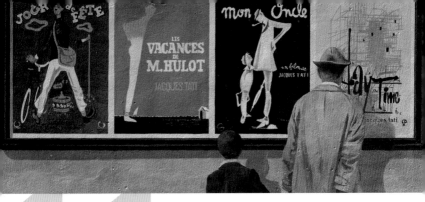

CANNES

The grand hotels and luxury shops of La Croisette make Cannes a magnet for hedonists and the jet set, but a walk around town also reveals a lively food market and picturesque old quarter.

DISTANCE 4.5km (2¾ miles)
TIME Two or three hours
START Palais des Festivals
END Vieux Port
POINTS TO NOTE
Park in the car park near Marché Forville or the one under the Palais des Festivals. From the train station, turn right on rue Jean Jaurès and descend rue Jean de Riouffé to the Palais des Festivals. If you do not want to shop or visit the museum, then this is also a good walk to do in the evening, when boulevard de la Croisette is colourfully illuminated and the people-watching is as good as by day.

Below: Palais des Festivals, focal point of the Film Festival.

Food and Drink
① CAFFÉ ROMA
1 square Merimée; tel: 04 93 38 05 04; daily L and D; €€
The terrace at this big café is popular day and night for an espresso, cocktails, pasta or simply the ringside view of comings and goings from the Palais des Festivals.

For a town now inextricably associated with film-festival glamour, Cannes had modest origins as a dependency of the monks of Lérins. It remains a town of intriguing contrasts, where show-off La Croisette contrasts with villagey Le Suquet where men play *boules* under the trees in front of the town hall.

PALAIS DES FESTIVALS

Begin at the **Palais des Festivals** ❶, which occupies centre stage on the seafront between the Old Port and La Croisette. Although the 1980s building, nicknamed 'the bunker', is uninspiring, it plays a leading role in the drama of the annual two-week Film Festival. Be sure to re-enact the famous climb up the red-carpeted stairs – a photo opportunity not to be missed – and follow the trail of handprints left by actors and directors in the terracotta esplanade below. Despite its 18 auditoria used for a panoply of music industry, advertising and property fairs, luxury tourism and shopping conventions, rock concerts and gala spectacles, there are plans afoot for an expansion and modernisation. The building also contains the **Croisette Casino** (www.lucienbarriere.com) and the **Tourist Office** *(see p.105)*. Cross the street to spy on the action from **Caffé Roma**, see ⑪①, before heading eastwards along boulevard de la Croisette.

LA CROISETTE

Cannes' palm-tree-lined seafront boulevard is a mix of glitz and grandeur, with ritzy hotels, luxury boutiques and a constant parade of open-topped cars. In summer the long sandy beach is almost entirely taken up by private beach concessions, with restaurants, deckchairs and jetties for parascending and water-skiing. Even in winter you will see leathery-skinned ladies bronzing in bikinis, at the same time as others promenade in fur coats up above.

Nonstop designer labels and jewellers at the start of La Croisette provide

Above from far left: mural celebrating French cinema; view from La Croisette.

Beaches
Plage de la Croisette is almost entirely taken up by private beach concessions and restaurants, although there is a small, busy public section between the Majestic jetty and the Palais des Festivals. If you do not want to pay for a private beach, it is better to head for the Plage du Midi at La Bocca, west of Port Vieux, or the Plage du Mourré Rouge on the eastern side of town.

While the official Film Festival each May is strictly reserved for film industry professionals and the press, there are opportunities to see films during the festival. Cinéma de la Plage holds free screenings on the beach, while tickets for the Quinzaine des Réalisateurs (www.quinzaine-realisateurs.com) go on sale at La Malmaison, with screenings in various cinemas around town.

great window-shopping. At no. 10, the first of Cannes' triumvirate of grand palace hotels is the **Majestic**, which opened in 1926; it keeps up to date with trendy DJs at its fashionable beach restaurant. Stretching between no. 17 and rue d'Antibes, the **Gray d'Albion shopping mall** offers evening wear, haute jewellery and kids' designer togs.

Detour up rue du Commandant André, where the quadrangle formed with rue des Frères Pradignac and rue du Dr Monod is a focus for nightlife. Many bars, such as **Via Notte**, see ⑪②, open only in the evening, but Provençal restaurant **La Mère Besson**, see ⑪③, is a prized address at lunch as well.

Grands Hôtels

Back on La Croisette, **La Malmaison** ❷ (no. 47; tel: 04 97 06 44 90; July–mid-Sept Tue–Sun 11am–8pm, mid-Sept–Apr Tue–Sun 10am–1pm and 2–6pm; charge) is the former tearoom of the original 19th-century Grand Hôtel, which was replaced by a tower in the 1960s; it is now used for art exhibitions. Further along, limos pull up at **Hôtel Palais Princesse Stéphanie**, site of the original Palais des Festivals and still a favourite for festival press conferences.

At no. 58, the **Carlton Interconti-nental**, opened in 1912, accommodates the Film Festival jury. The cupolas at either end of its façade were supposedly modelled on the voluptuous breasts of celebrated courtesan La Belle Otero. At no. 73, the Art Deco **Martinez** was France's largest hotel when it opened in 1929 with 476 master bedrooms and 56 bedrooms for clients' personal staff.

AROUND RUE D'ANTIBES

From here La Croisette continues past sun-seeking apartment blocks to Port Canto marina and Pointe de la Croisette. It is more interesting, though, to retrace your steps and take rue Pasteur to **rue d'Antibes** ❸. The street, which follows the former royal carriage route between Toulon and Antibes, is almost entirely dedicated to shopping, mixing mainstream fashion chains with younger, cutting-edge designers. Look up to see fine late 19th-century sculptures, rotundas and wrought-iron decoration, along with remnants of old shopfronts, some of which were once aimed at Cannes' British residents.

The Discovery of Cannes

In 1834, when an outbreak of cholera prevented British Lord Chancellor Henry Brougham from getting to Italy, he back-tracked to the small fishing village of Cannes, where he put up at the simple Hôtel de la Poste (today indicated by a plaque at 4 rue du Port). He liked it so much he stayed, buying a plot of land and building the neoclassical Villa Eléonore on what is now avenue Dr Picard. Cannes' future as an aristocratic winter destination was made. To see some of the villas of the early settlers, explore La Croix des Gardes district west of Le Suquet; the Villa Rothschild (1 avenue Jean de Noailles), set in lovely gardens, is now the municipal library, and Château de la Tour (10 avenue Font-de-Veyre) a comfortable hotel.

Rue du Bivouac Napoléon

Turn left down rue des Belges and right into **rue du Bivouac Napoléon**, where Napoleon camped out on 1 March 1815, having landed at Golfe-Juan after his escape from exile on Elba. The street today has some relaxed cafés and the **Cannes English Bookshop** at no. 11, a useful source of holiday reading.

ALLÉES DE LA LIBERTÉ

At the end of rue du Bivouac Napoléon, place General Charles de Gaulle opens onto the **Allées de la Liberté** ❹, with its vintage bandstand, *pétanque* pitches and morning **flower market** (Tue–Sun). On the northern side, rue Félix Faure is lined with bars and brasseries, notably seafood institution **Astoux et Brun**, see ⑪④, and a marble **statue of Lord Henry Brougham** *(see feature box)* stands on a plinth above a very British-looking lion. On the opposite side is the **Vieux Port** (Old Port), where a few fishing boats sit somewhat incongruously among the luxury yachts.

MARCHÉ FORVILLE

Opposite the pompous 19th-century Hôtel de Ville (Town Hall), take rue Louis Blanc to **Marché Forville** ❺ (summer daily 7am–1pm, winter Tue–Sun), an animated covered market. In summer it is a feast of tomatoes, aubergines, green figs and piles of garlic, and you can sample *tapenades* and olive oils, although you have to arrive early to find what is left of the local catch.

Running parallel, rue Meynadier is busy with inexpensive clothes and beach gear stores at its eastern end plus some simple restaurants, including **Aux Bons Enfants**, see ⑪⑤, nearer the market.

Above from far left: Carlton's façade; Marché Forville.

Food and Drink 🍴

② VIA NOTTE
13 rue du Commandant André; tel: 04 92 98 62 82; www.vianotte.fr; daily 6pm–2.30am
This stylish newcomer on the nightlife scene has quickly made its mark as a place for an early evening cocktail around its high outdoor tables or as a pre-club venue with DJs inside later on.

③ LA MÈRE BESSON
13 rue des Frères Pradignac; tel: 04 93 39 59 24; Mon–Sat L and D; €€
Remaining resolutely traditional amid a cluster of trendy lounge bars, the Mother Besson has been serving up Provençal specialities for over half a century.

④ ASTOUX ET BRUN
27 avenue Félix Faure; tel: 04 93 39 21 87; www.astoux brun.com; daily L and D; €€
This eternally popular seafood brasserie behind the port is a magnet as much for the superb people-watching as for its big platters of shellfish and it serves food throughout the day. Takeaway dishes are also available.

⑤ AUX BONS ENFANTS
80 rue Meynadier; no tel; Mon–Sat L and D; €
A simple bistro near to the market, which has been in the same family since 1934 and serves comforting regional home cooking, such as grilled sardines and herby Sisteron lamb with courgettes or Swiss chard. No credit cards.

Above from left:
eating out in Le
Suquet; Grasse.

Ile Ste-Marguerite
The larger of the two
Iles de Lérins offers
quiet beaches and
creeks, shady woods
and the Fort Royal,
where the Musée de
la Mer contains items
like amphorae from
Roman shipwrecks
and the heavily barred
cell of the mysterious
Man in the Iron Mask.
Boats leave from Quai
Laubeuf with Horizon
(tel: 04 92 98 71 36)
or Trans Côte d'Azur
(tel: 04 92 98 71 30).

Below: Notre Dame
de l'Espérance.

LE SUQUET

At its western end rue Meynadier climbs into rue St-Antoine, start of the picturesque Old Town. Before the arrival of the British in the 19th century, **Le Suquet** was pretty much all there was of Cannes: a few narrow streets and stepped alleyways of tall, yellow and pink houses that still wind up the hill to the fortress constructed by the monks of Lérins. The district is lively at night, when visitors flock to the bars and restaurants on rue St-Antoine and its continuation rue du Suquet.

Notre-Dame de l'Espérance

At place du Suquet turn left up rue Coste-Corail, and then take the traverse de l'Église. This brings you out at the big 17th-century church **Notre-Dame de l'Espérance ❻**, a late example of Provençal Gothic, with a plain, almost unadorned stone façade; the adjoining clock tower is a local landmark. In front, the square is used

for concerts in Les Nuits Musicales du Suquet *(see p.22)*. Continue round the side of the church to shady **place de la Castre**, which offers a fine view from its fortified wall.

Musée de la Castre

Entered through a pretty garden at the end of the square, the cool, white-washed rooms of the former castle of the monks of Lérins now contain the **Musée de la Castre ❼** (tel: 04 93 38 55 26; Apr–June and Sept Tue–Sun 10am–1pm and 2–6pm, July–Aug daily 10am–7pm (Wed until 9pm), Oct–Mar Tue–Sun 10am–1pm and 2–5pm; charge). The ethnographic collection, donated by Dutchman Baron Lycklama in 1877, still has the atmosphere of a cabinet of curiosities, with an eclectic array of masks, head-dresses and ceremonial daggers from Tibet, Nepal and Ladakh, bone carvings from Alaska, animal-shaped jugs from Latin America and archaeological finds from Egypt, Cyprus and Mesopotamia. Musical instruments are displayed in the chapel, while three rooms overlooking the courtyard contain paintings by Orientalist and Provençal painters. In the courtyard is the **Tour du Suquet**, an 11th-century watchtower; the 109-step climb is rewarded by a panoramic view.

Return to the square; a right turn at the end of rue Perissol will take you into rue Mont Chevalier, which leads back to the Vieux Port.

GRASSE

With its challenging topography and the hard sell of the perfumeries on the outskirts of town, Grasse can be a difficult place to grasp. Yet the town merits exploration for its old centre, dynamic new perfume museum and the family home of the painter Fragonard.

Grasse grew up around its tanneries before becoming a centre of perfume production, and unlike much of the Riviera it is still essentially a manufacturing town. Grasse's prosperous perfume barons and middle classes hide out in smart *bastides* in the outskirts, leaving the old centre feeling rather abandoned and surprisingly run down.

Begin on cours Honoré Cresp, which was laid out as a promenade in the 19th century. Here the **Palais des Congrès** ❶, a former casino, now contains the **Tourist Office** (drop by here for information on perfume factory visits; *see p.105*) and congress centre.

MUSÉE INTERNATIONAL DE LA PARFUMERIE

Just up the hill, the recently expanded **Musée International de la Parfumerie** ❷ (2 boulevard du Jeu de Ballon; tel: 04 97 05 58 00; www.museesdegrasse.com; June–Sept 10am–7pm, Oct–May Wed–Mon 11am–6pm; charge) displays the assorted plants, minerals, roots and animal matter used for perfumes. A glasshouse contains olfactory plants and materials to sniff and touch. There is

also a vast collection of ancient and modern perfume bottles, along with a reconstructed medieval apothecary's shop, Marie-Antoinette's travelling case, early make-up, and various stills, alambics and equipment used in the distillation, 'enfleurage' and blending of perfume essences.

RUE JEAN OSSOLA

At the exit turn left from boulevard Honoré Cresp into **rue Jean Ossola**, the main thoroughfare of medieval

---

DISTANCE 1.5km (1 mile)
TIME Two or three hours
START Palais des Congrès
END Villa Musée Fragonard
POINTS TO NOTE
Grasse has a complicated one-way system, so leave your car in the car park on cours Honoré Cresp. Apart from Fragonard's 'Historic Factory', the main perfume factories (Fragonard, Galimard and Molinard) are located outside the town centre, as are the town's best restaurants.

Below: perfume in production in Grasse.

Grasse. It is lined with some fine *hôtels particuliers* that reveal the social aspirations of the town's wealthy burgers.

On the corner, **Café des Musées**, see ⑪①, is ideal for a drink or light meal. Across the street at no. 2 is the **Musée Provençal du Costume et du Bijou ❸** (tel: 04 93 36 44 65; Easter–Oct daily 10am–1pm and 2–6pm, Nov–Easter Mon–Sat; free), an attractively presented private collection of 18th- and 19th-century regional costumes and jewellery. A few doors up at no. 14 is the fine doorway of the **Hôtel Luce**, where swashbuckling musketeer d'Artagnan is said to have stayed.

Take a short detour up **impasse des Soeurs**, on the left, to the near derelict-looking medieval house where Queen Catherine de Médicis, responsible for introducing the Italian fashion for perfumed gloves into France *(see margin, left)*, stayed in the 16th century.

AROUND THE CATHEDRAL

Backtrack to rue Jean Ossola and take rue Gazan to place du Petit Puy. On the left is a square fortified watchtower, and at the rear of the square is the 12th-century **Cathédrale Notre-Dame-du-Puy ❹** (July–Sept daily 9.30–11.30am and 3–6pm, Oct–June Mon–Sat 9.30–11.30am and 3–5.30pm). The stark west front was altered in the 17th century, when two side doors were blocked up and the fanciful horseshoe-shaped staircase was added, but the gloomy interior is a heavy example of Provençal Romanesque with massive columns and cursory cross vaulting. To the right of the nave are three canvases by Rubens, while the transept contains some unusual sculptures of saints and a rare religious painting by Fragonard, *The Washing of the Feet* (1754).

Go through the arch to the left of the cathedral to **place du 24 Août**, a former cemetery with lovely views over the surrounding countryside.

Return through place Godeau and take the steps beside the Hôtel de Ville down to **place de l'Evêché**. At the back of the square, a fountain cascades down a row of arches that were originally cellars and warehouses. Cross rue de la

Poissonnerie through place Roustan into **rue Rêve Vieille** – named after a tax that used to be collected here – which has an eclectic mixture of medieval and 18th-century architecture.

PLACE AUX AIRES

Turn left at the end into rue Marcel Journet and right into rue de l'Oratoire, taking rue des Fabreries into the attractive **place aux Aires** ❺. Lined with tall, arcaded, mainly 16th- and 17th-century houses, the square was the original focus of the town's tanning industry. Today there's a small **food and flower market** (Tue–Sun). On a street leading off the western side is **La Voûte**, see ⑪②.

From the southern end, take rue Amiral de Grasse, home to antiques shops and upmarket clothes shops, which curves back to rue Jean Ossola.

USINE HISTORIQUE DE FRAGONARD

Return at the end to boulevard Fragonard for the **Usine Historique de Fragonard** ❻ (tel: 04 93 36 44 65; daily 9am–6pm (July–Aug until 7pm); free) at no. 20. Although most of the perfumes are now made at the modern Fabrique des Fleurs outside the centre, the factory founded by Eugène Fuchs in 1926 still makes and packages some perfumes, soaps and cosmetics, and contains a collection of antique stills and perfume bottles.

VILLA MUSÉE FRAGONARD

Continue down the boulevard, past the Jardin Publique, and through the gateway at no. 23 to the **Villa Musée Fragonard** ❼ (tel: 04 97 05 58 00; June–Sept daily 10am–6.30pm, Oct and Dec–May hours can vary), where Grasse-born painter Jean-Honoré Fragonard took refuge, having fled from Paris after the Revolution. The elegant 17th-century villa was one of the town's first *bastides*, built by local notables to escape the cluttered city centre. Inside are copies of a set of Fragonard's love scenes, artwork on themes favoured by Fragonard, and work by his niece Marguerite Gérard. Of greater interest is the stairwell with grisaille, trompe l'oeil paintings of Classical sculptures, and a peculiar blend of revolutionary and masonic symbols thought to be the work of Fragonard's son.

Above from far left: cathedral nave; Fragonard factory.

La Bastide du Parfumeur

This garden (979 Chemin des Gourettes, Mouans-Sartoux; tel: 04 92 98 92 69; www.labastide duparfumeur.com), just south of Grasse, puts an emphasis on biodiversity and traditional methods of cultivation. A flower garden arranged according to floral notes is followed by meadows where flowers are cultivated without fertilisers or pesticides.

Food and Drink

① CAFÉ DES MUSÉES
1 rue Jean Ossola; tel: 04 92 60 99 00; summer daily L and D, winter Mon–Sat L and D; €
This stylish modern café, conveniently located between the perfume and costume museums at the entrance to the Old Town, is ideal for a drink or a light lunch of salads, savoury tarts and home-made desserts.

② LA VOÛTE
3 rue de Thouron; tel: 04 93 36 11 43; daily L and D; €
A friendly, convivial restaurant, popular with locals as well as tourists, where Provençal specialities and meat roasted on an open fire are served in an atmospheric, two-tiered, vaulted room (hence the name) or on a terrace on place aux Aires.

ST-TROPEZ

The legendary Riviera resort of St-Tropez is a bewitching mix of Provençal fishing village and jet-setters' hotspot, with a handful of interesting museums and historical sights.

St-Trop on Screen

Roger Vadim's 1956 film *Et Dieu créa la femme* created both St-Trop's beach image and Brigitte Bardot, while in 1968, Alain Delon, Romy Schneider and a young Jane Birkin lazed around a pool in *La Piscine*. But for many French people St-Trop on film is inseparably associated with the elastic face of Louis de Funès in the series of cult comedies begun by *Les Gendarmes à Saint-Tropez* (1964).

DISTANCE 2.25km (1½ miles)
TIME Two or three hours
START/END Vieux Port
POINTS TO NOTE

The biggest problem with St-Tropez is the enormous summer traffic jams. If you do not have your own yacht for swanning into the Vieux Port or dropping anchor off the beach, use the ferry service from Ste-Maxime with Les Bâteaux Verts (tel: 04 94 49 29 39; www.bateauxverts.com), which runs several boats an hour in peak season. By car, try to use the back roads from Ramatuelle *(see p.95)* rather than the road from Ste-Maxime, and avoid aperitif hour and Tuesday and Saturday morning market days. The large car park along the Nouveau Port is just a short stroll from the Vieux Port.

St-Tropez continues to draw the international jet-set, combining, as it does, glamorous resort and authentic Provençal village. For all its showbiz flavour, de-luxe hotels, legendary nightlife, ostentatious yachts and sometimes outright vulgarity of the *m'as-tu vu* (see and be seen) scene, 'St-Trop' still has a surprising charm and even a certain democracy: anyone can dress up and parade along the quays, and those with the right look will be able to make it past the rigorous *physionomistes* (bouncers) of Les Caves du Roy.

VIEUX PORT

From early Roman martyr Torpes, who gave the town its name, via neo-Impressionist Paul Signac to today's party people, visitors have always arrived at St-Tropez by boat. The pretty **Vieux Port ❶** (Old Port) is still the town's animated heart, lined with tall, colourful houses that were faithfully restored after World War II damage, and busy quayside bars and brasseries.

Musée de l'Annonciade
Beside the port on place Grammont, the **Musée de l'Annonciade ❷** (tel:

Food and Drink

① **BAR DU PORT**

7 quai Suffren; tel: 04 94 97 00 54

A sleek, portside vantage point where a designer-clad crowd lounges in white and chrome sofas surveying the passers-by.

04 94 17 84 10; Sept, Oct and Dec–June Wed–Mon 10am–noon and 2–6pm, July–Aug daily 10am–1pm and 3–7pm; charge) is one of the region's best museums, with a collection of post-Impressionist and modern art focused on St-Tropez and the Riviera. Among the highlights are pointilliste views of St-Tropez by Signac, Nabis paintings by Vuillard and early Fauve works by Derain, Matisse and Braque.

Maison des Papillons

Cut through to rue Allard, with its boutiques and arcades, and detour up narrow rue Etienne Berny for another surprising museum, the **Maison des Papillons ❸** (tel: 04 94 97 63 45; Apr–Oct and Christmas hols Mon–Sat 2.30–6pm; charge), where over 4,000 species of butterfly collected by painter Dany Lartigue are displayed around a small

fisherman's house. The painter was the son of famous 1920s society photographer J.H. Lartigue, some of whose photos can be seen in the kitchen.

The Quays

Return to the port, where **quai Suffren** is the place in St-Tropez to people-watch. Luxury yachts moor sternside to the quay, allowing promenaders to gawp at uniformed flunkeys and onboard cocktail parties, while others try to look nonchalant from the row of portside bars, such as **Bar du Port**, see ❶①, and neo-Baroque Café de Paris.

Halfway along, in front of the Hôtel Sube, with its own discreetly fashionable bar on the first floor, is a statue of **Bailli de Suffren ❹** (1729–88), erected in 1866 using bronze from melted-down arms captured from the Royal Navy. One of St-Tropez's most illustrious

Above: yachts line the horizon at St-Trop's seafront.

Paul Signac

Pointilliste painter Signac discovered St-Tropez when he sailed into the small fishing port in 1892 in his yacht *Olympia*. Soon he had bought a house in the town to work in, capturing the port and bay with meticulous tiny points of colour on canvas that sometimes verged on simple geometrical bands, and inviting fellow artists including H.E. Cross, Matisse, Derain and Marquet to visit.

Above from left: sunbathing at Club 55; brightly painted St-Tropez boat; harbour.

Plage de Pampelonne

Located 6km (4 miles) south of town, the Plage de Pampelonne maintains St-Tropez's reputation for sex, sea and sun. Much of the long stretch of sand is taken up by 'private' beach clubs, varying from the boho bamboo shack to designer haunts offering cosmopolitan menus, cocktails, DJs and beauty treatments. Trendy spots include veteran showbiz haunt Tahiti, venerable Club 55, Kon Tiki with its wooden huts, the Nikki Beach, Voile Rouge, the simpler Tropicana and fish restaurant Chez Camille. However, there are also free public stretches where you can put up your parasol, and anyone can walk along the shorefront.

adopted citizens, Pierre-André de Suffren's nautical career culminated with a successful Indian campaign and the command of the French navy.

Further along, **Le Gorille**, see ⑪②, dispenses drinks and brasserie standards day and night. Opposite, next to the **Tourist Office** *(see p.105)*, a small arch leads to **place aux Herbes**, where there is a small **fish market** every morning.

A bigger attraction is the red chairs of **Senequier**, see ⑪③, on **quai Jean Jaurès**, perfect for people-watching at aperitif hour, and the elegant terraces of **Le Quai Joseph**, see ⑪④, and sister fish restaurant, Escale Joseph, a few doors up.

On **quai Frédéric Mistral** is a memorial to the navies of France, America and Britain and the Liberation of Provence; Allied forces landed on the Var coast on 15 August 1944.

La Glaye

Walk between the squat round **Tour du Portalet** and La Tour Joseph restaurant, where the beginning of the coast footpath leads over the rocks to **La Glaye ⑤**, a small cove surrounded by pastel-coloured fishermen's houses.

AROUND THE HÔTEL DE VILLE

From the beach, take the first of the covered archways into rue Sous de la Glaye, which comes out on **place de l'Hôtel de Ville**, where the Hôtel de Ville faces a fine mansion with a carved wooden doorway brought back from Zanzibar in the 1800s by a Tropezian navigator.

At the lower end of the square, the **Château de Suffren ⑥**, though now named after the naval hero, is a remnant of the square tower built by Guillaume, 1st Count of Provence, in 980. It was built to protect the Gulf of St-Tropez's settlements from North African Barbary pirates, whose raids plagued the region until the 15th century.

Take rue Sibille, then turn left up rue de l'Église to **Église Parossiale ⑦** (open morning only), St-Tropez's parish church, which contains a carved bust of St Torpes. Take rue du Clocher up the side of the church through place de l'Ormeau and rue de l'Ormeau into rue de la Citadelle, where the triangular rough stone **Tour Jarlier** is a remaining corner of the town ramparts.

CITADELLE

At the top of rue de la Citadelle, steps lead across the Pré des Pecheurs to the **Citadelle ⑧** (tel: 04 94 97 59 43; www. saint-tropez.fr; Apr–Sept daily 10am– 6.30pm, Oct–Mar daily 10am– 12.30pm and 1.30–5.30pm; charge), built in the early 17th century for King Henri IV. Although it was the principal coastal defence between Antibes and Toulon, the fortress was nonetheless attacked by Spanish troops in 1637. In 1652 its garrison joined La Fronde rebellion against the king, and the townspeople, aided by royal troops from Toulon, besieged the castle. The Naval Museum housed in the hexagonal keep is currently closed for renovation (due to reopen 2012 at the earliest); in the meantime, ramparts lined with cannons and the roof terrace of the keep provide fine views over the town and bay.

AROUND PLACE DES LICES

Return to rue de la Citadelle, and at place Forbin turn left along rue du Petit Bal and descend rue de la Miséricorde, marked by the tiled dome of the **Chapelle de la Miséricorde**, into **rue Gambetta**. Here, elegant 18th-century doorways of shipowners' and merchants' houses punctuate upmarket shops, such as **Villebrequin** (nos 24 and 28), homegrown seller of men's swimming trunks.

Continue to **place des Lices ❾**. The big square is where St-Tropez millionaires play at being Provençal villagers, renting *boules* from the **Café des Lices**, see ⑪⑤, for a game of *pétanque* under the plane trees and congregating at the *très chic* **food and general market** on Tuesday and Saturday mornings.

Return to the Vieux Port along **rue Georges Clemenceau**, source of St-Trop's classic strappy centurion sandals from **Atelier Rondini** (no.16), cream-filled cakes at **La Tarte Tropezienne** (no.36), and celeb chef Christophe Leroy's **Table du Marché**, see ⑪⑥, a tempting bistro, snack bar and tearoom.

Food and Drink

② LE GORILLE

1 quai Suffren; 04 94 97 03 93; www.legorille.com; July and Aug daily 24 hours, Sept–June daily 8am–1am; €
Compared with its designer neighbours, the open-all-hours Gorilla is a refreshingly down-to-earth place serving coffees, steak tartare and *salade niçoise* all day, and sustenance for après-clubbers all night long.

③ SENEQUIER

Quai Jean Jaurès; tel: 04 94 97 20 20; www.senequier. com; end-Feb–early Jan daily B, L and D; €€
This St-Tropez institution, which opened as a patisserie specialising in nougat in 1887 (still available at 4 place aux Herbes), has had a recent makeover but happily has kept the rows of red directors' chairs for surveying the portside scene. Not cheap but a must at aperitif time.

④ LE QUAI JOSEPH

22 quai Jean Jaurès; tel: 04 94 97 04 07; www.joseph-saint-tropez.com; daily L and D; €€€
The ubiquitous Joseph now has six restaurants and bars around town. This one goes for fashionable Japanese and Indo-Chinese fusion (sushi, sashimi and wok dishes). Sit in white tub chairs sunk into artificial black sand on the terrace or opt for the sultry zebra-stripe lounge bar inside.

⑤ CAFÉ DES LICES

Place des Lices; 04 94 97 44 69; www.lecafe.fr; daily L and D; €€
A classic café, serving up grilled steaks and Provençal specialities to generations of celebs. Sit on the terrace or in the vintage interior or rent a set of *boules* for a game of *pétanque* on the square.

⑥ TABLE DU MARCHÉ

38 rue Georges Clemenceau; tel: 04 97 85 20; www. christophe-leroy.com; daily L and D; €€
The relaxed bistro of celeb chef Christophe Leroy. At the front, 'le snack' serves up quiches, tarts and delicious patisseries; at the rear, the bistro has a Franco-Mediterranean menu scanning dishes like beef fillet with morels, duck magret, risotto and pasta.

MASSIF DES MAURES

A circular driving tour through the wild mountain hinterland of St-Tropez and the scenic Corniche coast road, with footpaths, monasteries, beaches, vineyards and tropical gardens to discover en route.

DISTANCE Approximately 95km (60 miles)

TIME A full day

START Cogolin

END Domaine de Rayol

POINTS TO NOTE

Cogolin is on the D98 (former N98) which links Hyères in the west with St-Tropez in the east. Distances on this tour are not far as the crow flies, but allow plenty of time as some of the mountain roads are hair-raisingly twisty and narrow.

All in a Name

The Massif des Maures gets its name from *maurus* (the Provençal word for sombre or dark brown), relating to the dark colour of the hills rather than the Moors who occupied them for much of the Middle Ages.

Guided Walks

The Office National de Forêts organises guided walks in the heart of the Massif des Maures, exploring varied facets from prehistoric menhirs to flora and fauna; you can get information and make reservations at the tourist offices in Bormes-les-Mimosas (tel: 04 94 01 38 38), Collobrières (tel: 04 94 48 08 00) and La Garde Freinet (tel: 04 94 43 67 41).

Just minutes from the family-oriented resort of Le Lavandou or the bustle of St-Tropez is the thickly forested and surprisingly wild mountains of the Massif des Maures. Timber, chestnut and cork production are still the main activities here, and forestry roads and long-distance footpaths provide numerous opportunities for hiking.

COGOLIN AND GRIMAUD

After the showbiz antics of St-Tropez, **Cogolin ❶** has the appeal of a real working town, with useful facilities such as a petrol station and supermarket, and home-grown industries (briar pipe and carpet making). Also here is the pretty 11th-century church and the **Musée Raimu** (18 avenue Georges Clemenceau; tel: 04 94 54 18 00; www. musee-raimu.com; July–Aug Mon–Sat 10am–noon and 4–7pm, Sun 4–7pm, Sept–June Mon and Wed–Sat 10am–noon and 3–6pm, Sun 3–6pm; charge), a shrine to actor Raimu, containing photos, costumes and memorabilia from his roles in Marcel Pagnol's classic films *Marius* (1931) and *César* (1936).

Now take the D558 3.5km (2 miles) north to **Grimaud ❷**, a hill village with a tangle of pretty streets sitting under a set of picturesque castle ruins.

LA GARDE FREINET

Continue northwest for 9km (5½ miles) through gnarled cork oak woods; look out for trees where the lower section of the trunk has been stripped of its bark for cork production, once the principal activity of **La Garde Freinet ❸**. This small, lively town is home to an attractive main square with a fountain, cafés and a couple of sophisticated homeware shops. It grew up in the 13th century,

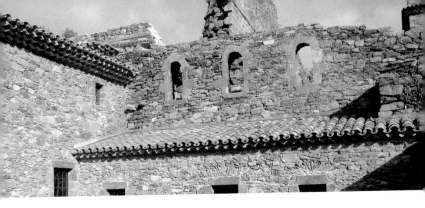

when the population moved down from the hilltop settlement that had developed around the Saracen fortress of **Fraxinet**, a steep walk to the northwest.

Return to Grimaud and head west towards Collobrières along the D14.

CHARTREUSE DE LA VERNE

After 20km (12 miles), turn left onto the narrow D214, which climbs up through dense woodland. Leave your car at the car park and continue on foot up to the forbidding, fortress-like Carthusian monastery of the **Chartreuse de la Verne ❹** (tel: 04 94 48 08 00; Wed–Mon 11am–5pm (June–Aug until 6pm), closed in periods of high fire risk; charge). Founded in 1170 by the Bishop of Toulon, it sits brooding on the hillside in solitary splendour. Apart from the Romanesque church, most of the buildings date from the 17th century and have been rebuilt on several occasions due to fire damage. Abandoned after the Revolution, restoration work began in the 1970s and since 1983 the monastery has been resettled by a community of nuns. The visit begins

Above from far left: Grimaud; Chartreuse de la Verne.

Forest Fires

Forest fires are a constant threat to the region in the hot, dry summers. Sadly, they are often caused by arson or started by accident; you may find some of the roads and footpaths closed off at times of high risk, especially during high winds.

Above from left:
touring the mountains
of the Massif des
Maures; flower detail
in Domaine du Royal;
view from the Cor-
niche des Maures.

in the massive gatehouse, taking in the church, cloister, cemetery, grainstore and a restored monk's cell with a private courtyard for meditation.

COLLOBRIÈRES

Return to the D14, where the road continues along the Réal Collobrier valley to **Collobrières ⑤**. The town thrived in the 19th century with the logging industry, and cork oak and chestnut cultivation, when timber barons put up fine houses and the medieval Église de St-Pons was supplanted by a new neo-Gothic edifice. Today, the small, pleasant town is renowned for its sweet chestnuts and has an 11th-century humpbacked bridge, attractive old streets and a string of simple restaurants, such as the **Hôtel-Restaurant des Maures**, see ⑪①.

COL DE BABAOU

About 2 km (1 mile) after leaving Collobrières, turn left on the D41 towards Bormes-les-Mimosas. The narrow road winds up endless hairpin bends to the **Col de Babaou ⑥** pass at 414m (1,360ft), with fine views of the sea and Iles de Hyères in one direction and the Laquin peak in the other. Some 8km (5 miles) further on at the Col de Gratteloup the road crosses the busy D98. Continue along the D41, which descends into the pretty village of Bormes-les-Mimosas.

BORMES-LES-MIMOSAS

Built strategically on a hill inland from the coast, under the remains of the castle of the Lords of Fos, the village of **Bormes-les-Mimosas ⑦** is swathed not just in mimosa, but in colourful bougainvillea and artfully planted agaves and cactuses. Village life centres on the animated place Gambetta, with its cafés and restaurants, such as **La Tonnelle**, see ⑪②. It leads to the craft and food shops of rue Carnot and other atmospheric streets like rue Ruompi Cuuo.

Food and Drink 🍴

① HÔTEL-RESTAURANT DES MAURES
19 boulevard Lazare Carnot, Collobrières; tel: 04 94 48 07 10; daily L and D; €
A popular, unpretentious, family-run restaurant with tables on the terrace spanning the Réal Collobrier river. Sustaining rustic fare includes a fine wild boar stew.

② LA TONNELLE
23 place Gambetta, Bormes-les-Mimosas; tel: 04 94 71 34 84; www.la-tonnelle-bormes.com; July and Aug daily D, May, June and Sept Fri–Tue L and D, Thur D, Oct–mid Nov and mid-Dec–Apr Fri–Tue L and D; €€
In a stylish dining room on Bormes' main square, chef Gil Renard cooks up superb modern Provençal fare, combining regional produce with a well-judged use of spices.

③ MAURIN DES MAURES
Boulevard du TCF, Le Rayol Canadel; tel: 04 94 05 60 11; www.maurin-des-maures.com; daily L and D; €€
This noisy, animated institution combines a popular restaurant where you are packed in at long communal tables, and a local bar-tabac with pinball and babyfoot (table football). Come for fish soup, Provençal classics and great desserts. Reservations are recommended.

CAP DE BREGANÇON BEACHES

From Bormes descend to the coast by the boulevard du Soleil, turning right through Le Pin. At the roundabout take the D559 towards Le Lavandou. After about 200m/yds, detour right down route de Cabassol towards **Cap de Brégançon** for the best beaches in the area. At the end of the road, turn right (west) passing the cream-coloured wine-producing Château de Brégançon, then turn left to the **Plage de l'Estagnol** ❽ (Easter–Oct; parking charge), a beautiful shallow sandy cove with shady pines and the excellent **Resto Plage de l'Estagnol** (tel: 04 94 64 71 11; Apr–Sept daily L and D; reserve for dinner); alternatively, turn left (east) for the **Plage du Cabasson** (parking charge) and the Fort de Brégançon, one of the official residences of the French president, which sits on its own guarded peninsula.

Return to the D559. At rondpoint (roundabout) de la Baou take the route de Benat and then turn left on avenue de la Mer to Bormes' beach suburb of **La Favière**, which has a long beach of fine golden sand and a marina offering good diving, kayaking and sailing facilities.

LE LAVANDOU

La Favière runs into the family-friendly resort of **Le Lavandou** ❾, where a rather glitzy seafront promenade and long, crowded sandy beach hide a surprisingly pretty little Old Town. At the eastern end of the harbour, the road tunnel brings you back to the D559. A little further on to the right, the curved, steeply shelving beach at St-Clair is the nicest of Le Lavandou's beaches.

DOMAINE DU RAYOL

From here the D559 Corniche des Maures follows the coast eastwards, through Cavalière and up towards the Pointe de la Chappe at Rayol-Canadel, past **Maurin-des-Maures**, see ⑪③.

Follow signs to the right for the fabulous gardens of the **Domaine du Rayol** ❿ (avenue des Belges, Le Rayol-Canadel; tel: 04 98 04 44 00; www.domaindurayol.org; daily 9.30am–7.30pm; charge), created in 1910 by banker Alfred Courmes, who filled the grounds around his house with exotic plants. The Domaine now belongs to the Conservatoire du Littoral coastal trust, which restored the gardens and added species from other Mediterranean-type climates in Australia, southern California, Mexico and Cape Horn. Pick up the leaflet to follow a trail with giant ferns, Australian blackboys and other unusual plants. There is even an underwater *jardin marin* to be visited with snorkel and flippers (guided visit by reservation), as well as classical concerts in summer.

From here you can head to St-Tropez on the D559, or turn right at **La Croix Valmer** (13km/8 miles) to **Gassin** and **Ramatuelle** *(see margin)*.

St-Tropez Peninsula
If you have time to spare, detour via the scenic hilltop village of Gassin and then take the D89 towards Ramatuelle. Here the landscape becomes more open, with red sandy soils and vineyards producing some good Côtes de Provence wines.

Originally a Saracen stronghold, Ramatuelle is a chic place for an evening out from St-Tropez, with its restaurants and summer jazz and theatre festivals. Pause for a coffee at casually chic Café de l'Ormeau before going through the fortified gateway next to the church to explore the Old Town.

Below the town, the D93 (route des Plages) loops around the peninsula, with side roads branching off towards the legendary beach clubs of Plage de Pampelonne *(see p.90)*, before it rejoins the D98 to St-Tropez.

DIRECTORY

A user-friendly alphabetical listing of practical information, plus hand-picked hotels and restaurants, clearly organised by area, to suit all budgets and tastes. Select nightlife listings are also included here.

A

AGE RESTRICTIONS

Minimum ages: consent 15, marriage 18, buying alcohol 16, drinking wine or beer in a bar 16, drinking spirits in a bar 18, driving 18.

B

BUDGETING

Expect to pay €3.50 for a 25cl *(un demi)* of draught lager and €4–7 for a glass of house wine. A main course in a budget restaurant will cost €10–15, in a moderate one €18–25 and in an expensive one €45–60. A double room in a cheap hotel will cost around €60, in a moderate one €140 and in a deluxe hotel €400. A single bus ticket in Nice costs €1, a one-day bus pass €4.

C

CHILDREN

Most hotels have family rooms or suites that can sleep three or four, or can add a folding bed in a double room. Children are always accepted in restaurants; children's menus – where available – are often variations on burgers, sausages, fish and chips or pasta, and ice cream; some chefs will prepare special dishes.

In France, children generally get in free to museums, although the age varies from under 12s to under 18s; the permanent collections of national museums are free for under 26s; Nice's municipal museums are free for everyone.

CLOTHING

Cannes, Monaco and St-Tropez are the Riviera's dressiest places, although only the grandest restaurants and casinos require gentlemen to wear a jacket and tie *(tenue correcte)*. In general, think 'smart-casual' – avoid shorts for dining out at night and trainers if you want to get into exclusive nightclubs. A lot of attention is paid to accessories: the right sandals, sunglasses or bag can make all the difference. Try not to wander around the streets in swimwear; in Monaco it is formally forbidden and respectable attire is required for religious buildings.

Even in summer, a sweater, wrap or light jacket is useful for cooler evenings, and a waterproof coat or jacket will be needed from October to April. For climate information, *see p.11.*

CRIME AND SAFETY

Such a prosperous region inevitably attracts petty criminals, but incidents of violent crime against visitors are rare. Do not carry lots of cash, never leave valuables in your car, and look out for pickpockets, especially in crowds; in Nice, be careful of bags or watches snatched through open car windows when waiting at traffic lights Any loss or theft should be reported immediately to the nearest *commissariat de police*.

CUSTOMS

As France is part of the EU, free exchange of non-duty-free goods for personal use is permitted between France and the UK and the Republic of Ireland. If you go to the very popular Friday street market in Ventimiglia (Ventimille in French) just across the border in Italy, be careful about buying counterfeit goods; customs checks are frequent at the Menton border post and you could be prosecuted.

For residents of non-EU countries, restrictions on bringing goods into France are as follows: 200 cigarettes or 50 cigars or 250g tobacco, 1 litre of spirits and 2 litres of wine. Non-EU residents can claim a refund *(détaxe)* of TVA (VAT) on certain goods, such as clothes, if they spend more than €175 in one shop on one day. Ask for a *bordereau de vente à l'exportation*, which should be stamped by customs on leaving and then posted back to the shop.

DISABLED TRAVELLERS

Disabled access can be difficult in historic buildings or the stepped streets of old hill towns, but many of the south's recently renovated museums do have wheelchair access. All hotels built since 1978 should have at least one specially adapted bedroom, while public buildings constructed since 1978 should also be accessible. The Association des Paralysés de France (www.apf.asso.fr) produces an annual *Guide Vacances*. A Tourisme & Handicap classification (www.tourisme-handicaps.org) is gradually being introduced to show facilities accessible for visitors with physical, visual, hearing or learning difficulties.

E

ELECTRICITY

220-volt, 50-cycle AC is universal, generally with a three-pin plug. British visitors will need an adaptor *(adaptateur)*; American visitors will need a transformer *(transformateur)*.

EMBASSIES AND CONSULATES

Australia: (embassy) 4 rue Jean-Rey, 75015 Paris; tel: 01 40 50 33 00; www. france.embassy.gov.au.
Canada: (consulate) 35 avenue Montaigne, 75008 Paris; tel: 01 44 43 29 02; www.international.gc.ca.
Republic of Ireland: (embassy) 12 avenue Foch, 75116 Paris; tel: 01 44 17 67 00; www.embassyofirelandparis.com.
UK: (consulate) 24 avenue du Prado, 13006 Marseille; tel: 04 91 15 72 10; http://ukinfrance.free.gov.uk.

Above from far left: Monaco Aquarium; Niki de Saint Phalle's *Loch Ness Monster* fountain outside the Théâtre National de Nice.

Kids' Fun
Nice's beach is pebbly, but some private concessions have sandpits and children's pools. Otherwise, Antibes, Bormes-les-Mimosas and Le Lavandou all have sandy beaches. Nice also has lots of small garden-square playgrounds in the New Town, plus the Parc Floral Phoenix (www.nice. fr/environnement/ parc-phoenix). In Antibes, Marineland (www.marineland.fr) has animal shows and a waterpark, while St-Jean-Cap-Ferrat has a small zoo. There is an aquarium in Monaco's Musée Océanographique, plus dolls in the Musée National and vintage cars in the Collection des Voitures Anciennes. Both Monaco and Cannes have firework displays in summer.

US: (consulate) 7 avenue Gustave V, 06000 Nice; tel: 04 93 88 89 55; http://france.usembassy.gov/consulara.html.

EMERGENCIES

Ambulance: 15
Police: 17
Fire brigade *(sapeurs–pompiers)*: 18 (will also answer medical emergencies)

Dial 112 from a mobile phone for all emergencies.

ETIQUETTE

Madame/Mademoiselle and *Monsieur* are widely used in French. Unless you know someone well or are talking to children, use the formal *vous* rather than *tu* form. It is polite to shake hands when meeting someone. Do not kiss cheeks with someone you do not know, unless they propose to 'donne la bise'; a polite peck on either cheek. And note that topless bathing (very in during the 1980s and 1990s) has gone totally out of fashion. For clothing, *see p.98*.

G

GAY/LESBIAN ISSUES

France is generally gay tolerant. Nice and Cannes have several gay bars and clubs; Coco Beach east of Nice's Vieux Port is a popular gay beach. *Nice Practical Guide* and *www Cannes*, published by the respective tourist offices, list gay and gay-friendly bars and hotels. There's a lively Gay Pride parade in June in Nice.

GREEN ISSUES

Despite the huge potential for solar energy, France has been slow to take it up, with general reliance on state-generated nuclear energy, and there are limitations on use of solar panels in picturesque listed villages. However, most towns have recycling schemes for glass and newspapers and many hotels try to promote environmental awareness by conserving water and encouraging guests not to change towels every day. For information on carbon-offsetting your flights, *see margin, right*.

H

HEALTH

Healthcare is generally of an extremely high standard in France and the Côte d'Azur has the highest concentration of specialist doctors in France outside Paris. There are no compulsory vaccinations or particular health risks. Tap water is safe to drink, unless marked *eau non potable*. However, be careful to avoid sunburn; wear a sunhat and avoid exposure to the powerful midday sun. Other potential

Above from far left: buying sunflowers on the Cours Saleya in Nice; St-Tropez.

hazards are mosquitoes (many people use plug-in anti-mosquito diffusers) and, in some years, invasions of jellyfish *(méduses)* in the sea.

EU nationals can use the French Social Security system, which refunds up to 70 percent of medical expenses. British nationals should obtain a European Health Insurance Card before leaving the UK (www.ehic.org.uk). If you are ill, your hotel can probably recommend an English-speaking doctor or dentist; make sure it is a *médecin conventionné* (affiliated to the social security system). You will get a prescription and a *feuille de soins* (statement of treatment), allowing you to claim back part of the cost upon your return.

Nationals of non-EU countries should take out travel and medical insurance before leaving home.

Pharmacies and Hospitals

Pharmacies (indicated by a green cross) can provide basic medicaments and deal with minor ailments. The name and address of duty chemists open on Sunday and at night is displayed in pharmacies; the police station or local papers will also have it. There is an all-night pharmacy in Nice at 7 rue Masséna.

24-hour casualty departments *(urgences).* Centre Hospitalier Universitaire (CHU) St-Roch, 5 rue Piere Dévoluy, Nice; tel: 04 92 03 33 33. Centre Hôpitalier Princesse Grace, 1 avenue Pasteur, Monaco; tel: +377-97 98 97 69.

HOURS AND HOLIDAYS

Banks. Most banks are open Mon–Fri 9am–noon and 2–5pm; some open Saturday morning and close on Monday.
Museums. Major ones usually open 10am–5 or 6pm (later in summer) and often close on Monday or Tuesday; smaller museums often close for lunch.
Restaurants. These usually serve noon–2 or 2.30pm, 7.30 or 8pm–9.30 or 10pm, and may close one or two days a week; cafés and brasseries often open from early morning until late.
Shops. Shops generally open Mon–Sat 9.30 or 10am–7pm; small shops often take a long lunch break, closing at noon and reopening at 3 or 4pm; bakeries usually open 8am–8pm and may open on Sunday, closing another day a week; some supermarkets open till 9 or 10pm.

Public Holidays

1 Jan Nouvel An – New Year's Day
Mar/Apr Lundi de Pâques – Easter Monday
1 May Fête du Travail – Labour Day
8 May Fête de la Victoire 1945 – VE Day
May Ascension
May/June Lundi de Pentecôte – Whit Monday
14 July Fête Nationale – Bastille Day
15 Aug Assomption – Assumption
1 Nov Toussaint – All Saints' Day
11 Nov Anniversaire de l'Armistice – Armistice Day
25 Dec Noël – Christmas

Carbon-Offsetting
Air travel produces a huge amount of carbon dioxide and is a significant contributor to global warming. If you would like to offset the damage caused to the environment by your flight, a number of organisations can do this for you using online 'carbon calculators' that tell you how much you need to donate. In the UK visit www.climate care.org or www. carbonneutral.com; in the US log on to www.climatefriendly. com or www. sustainabletravel international.org.

I

INTERNET FACILITIES

Wi-fi is available in most hotels (often but not always free) and there are also hotspots in numerous cafés; Cannes is gradually installing a free Wi-fi network 'Cannes sans fil'. Many hotels also have a computer with internet access in the lobby. Tourist offices should be able to supply addresses of internet cafés.

L

LANGUAGE

The southern French accent draws out syllables and places extra emphasis on the ends of words or sentences. The usual nasal French 'en' ending becomes a hard 'ng' (*chien* sounds like *chieng*). In Vieux Nice you may see bilingual street names and hear Nissart, an old Occitan Provençal dialect that is experiencing a fashionable revival *(see p.13)*. French is the official language in Monaco, but Italian and English are also widely spoken; you may also come across Monégasque (an Italian dialect).

A list of useful words and phrases can be found on the pull-out map that accompanies this guide.

LEFT LUGGAGE

Since 9/11, security measures mean that only the largest train stations (Nice and Cannes) have left luggage facilities, with rather irregular hours. If you have an evening train or plane to catch, most hotels will store your luggage after checkout.

M

MAPS

Hotel and tourist offices can usually supply a town street map *(un plan)*. For driving, a 1:200,000 or 1:250,000 scale road atlas or sheet map *(carte routière)* of Provence Côte d'Azur is useful. For serious hiking, buy 1:25,000 scale maps published by IGN.

MEDIA

Newspapers. The British press is widely available in main cities and tourist destinations, as is *USA Today* and the Paris-based *International Herald Tribune*. Alongside French national dailies *Le Monde*, *Le Figaro* and *Libération*, the two main local newspapers are *Nice Matin* and *Var Matin*. Look out also for glossy expat magazine *Riviera Reporter* (www.riviera-reporter.com), which can also be downloaded, and monthly newspaper *The Riviera News*.

Radio. State radio stations include France Info, France Inter and France Musiques. Commercial stations include news-oriented Europe 1 and RTL, music stations NRJ and Nostalgie. Monaco's Riviera Radio broadcasts local news, sport and weather in English; frequencies vary across the region.

TV. The main TV channels are TF1, France 2, France 3, M6 and Arte; many hotels also have numerous cable and satellite channels, often including CNN, BBC World and Sky News.

MONEY

Currency. France is part of the eurozone. Banknotes are available in denominations of 500, 200, 100, 50, 20, 10 and 5 euros; avoid the largest denominations as many shops will not accept €200 and €500 notes. There are coins for 2 and 1 euros and for 50, 20, 10, 5, 2 and 1 cent.

Credit cards *(cartes de crédit)*. These are widely accepted, especially Visa and Mastercard. There may be a minimum sum (often €15).

Lost and stolen credit cards: American Express, tel: 01 47 77 72 00; Diners Club, tel: 0810 314 159; Eurocard/Mastercard, tel: 0800 901 387; Visa, tel: 0892 705 705.

Cash machines. ATMs are the simplest, and usually cheapest, way of obtaining cash in euros. They are plentiful in large cities, though may be scarce in rural areas.

Traveller's cheques. Traveller's cheques are rarely used; it is better to draw cash from a machine or use your credit card.

Tipping. A 10–15 per cent service charge is included in hotel and restaurant bills, so any further tip is optional, although rounding off bills with a few coins or small notes helps round off friendships with waiters, too. It is also in order to hand hotel porters, filling station attendants, etc, a coin or two for services.

P

POLICE

Theft should be reported to the Police Nationale in Nice (1 avenue Maréchal Foch, Nice; tel: 04 92 17 22 22) and Cannes or to the Gendarmerie in smaller towns and rural areas. Monaco has its own, highly visible, police force. Call 17 within France for police assistance.

POST

Post offices are indicated by a yellow 'La Poste' sign. When sending letters and small packages, it is often quicker to use the automatic stamp machines than to queue for service. *Tabacs* (tobacconists) also sell stamps. Letter boxes are yellow. It costs €0.56 to send a postcard or letter up to 20g within France, €0.70 to the EU and €0.85 to the rest of the world. Monaco stamps should be used to post letters from Monaco.

Nice's main post office, opposite the train station on avenue Thiers, is open Mon–Fri 8am–7pm and Sat 8am–noon; smaller post offices usually open Mon–Fri 9am–noon and 2–5pm, Sat 9am–noon.

Above from far left: Baie de Garavan, Menton; chillis at an outdoor produce market.

Lost Property
Lost property *(objets trouvés)* and lost passports should be reported to the police. The SNCF (French railways) has its own lost property system.
- Police Nationale, 1 avenue Maréchal Foch, Nice; tel: 04 92 17 22 22.
- SNCF, 1 rue Raoul Bosio, Nice; tel: 04 97 13 44 10.
- Commissariat de Police, 1 avenue de Grasse, Cannes; tel: 04 93 06 22 22.
- Direction de la Sûreté Publique, 3 rue Louis Notari, Monaco; tel: +377-93 15 30 15 (lost property, tel: +377-93 15 30 18).

R

RELIGION

The French Republic has officially been a lay state since the French Revolution and does not have an established religion; however, the church calendar determines most public holidays and the majority of the population is nominally Roman Catholic, with substantial minority Protestant, Muslim and Jewish communities. Non-Catholic services are called *cultes*; Protestant churches are known as *temples*. Roman Catholicism is the established religion in Monaco.

There are Anglican churches with regular services in English in Nice, Cannes, Menton, Monaco and Vence.

S

SMOKING

Smoking is prohibited in all state-owned buildings and public places, including post offices, stations, cinemas and museums, and on public transport. Since 1 January 2008 this has been extended to restaurants, bars, cafés, discothèques and casinos, except in specially ventilated, sealed-off *fumoirs* or outside on café terraces; smoking is banned in the public areas of hotels, but not in hotel bedrooms unless they are designated non-smoking rooms.

T

TELEPHONES

France uses a 10-digit telephone-number system. Numbers on the French Riviera begin with 04. Mobile phones start with 06; special-rate numbers varying from freephone 0800 to premium-rate 0892 start with 08. Directory enquiries are available from various providers, including 118000, 118007, 118008 and 118218.

When dialling France from abroad, dial the French country code 33 and omit the 0 at the start of the 10-digit number. To dial overseas from France, dial 00, followed by the country code (UK: 44; Canada and US: 1; Australia: 61; Monaco: 377) and then the number, usually omitting the initial zero.

Many public telephones only accept *télécartes* (phone cards), available from post offices and tobacconists. A surcharge will usually be added for calls made from your hotel room.

Mobile (cell) phones. If you are using a British-based mobile *(portable)* in France, dial as if you are a local subscriber. To call from one British phone to another, use the international code even if you are both in France.

TIME ZONES

France is one hour ahead of GMT and clocks go forward one hour between March and October.

TOILETS

There are free toilets in museums and department stores. If using a toilet in a café, it is polite to order at least a coffee at the bar.

TOURIST INFORMATION

Tourist offices *(offices de tourisme)* can provide maps and information on hotels, restaurants, sightseeing, festivals and tours and may have hotel reservation and ticket sales services. See also the tourist board websites for the Alpes-Maritimes (www.guiderivi era.fr), the Var (www.visitvar.fr) and Paca regional tourist board (www. decouverte-paca.fr).

Nice: 5 promenade des Anglais, tel: 08 92 70 74 07; www.nicetourisme.com; branches at Nice train station (avenue Thiers) and Aéroport Nice Côte d'Azur (T1).

Antibes: 11 place du Charles de Gaulle; tel: 04 97 23 11 11; www. antibes-juanlespins.com.

Cannes: Palais des Festivals, La Croisette; tel: 04 92 99 84 22; www. cannes-hotel-booking.com.

Grasse: 22 cours Honoré Cresp; tel: 04 93 36 66 66; www.grasse.fr.

Menton: Palais de l'Europe, 8 avenue Boyer; tel: 04 92 41 76 76; www. menton.fr.

Monaco: 2a boulevard des Moulins, Monte Carlo; tel: +377-92 16 61 16; www.visitmonaco.com.

St-Tropez: quai Jean Jaurès; tel: 08 92 68 48 28; www.ot-saint-tropez.com.

Vence: 8 place du Grand Jardin; tel: 04 93 58 06 38; www.vence.fr.

TRANSPORT

Arrival by Air

Aéroport Nice-Côte d'Azur (tel: 04 93 21 30 30; www.nice.aeroport.fr), on the western edge of Nice, is France's second busiest airport. Flights leave from two terminals, with scheduled connections from all major European cities, North Africa and some American cities.

RCA buses (www/rca.tm.fr) depart from Nice airport for main destinations along the coast: lines 23 (T1) and 99 (T1 and T2) serve Nice railway station *(gare SNCF)*; line 98 goes to Nice bus station *(gare routière)*; lines 110 Aéroport-Monte-Carlo-Menton Express and 210 Aéroport-Cannes Express are express services along the motorway. Buy tickets before boarding at the desks signposted 'Car Park/Bus Cash' inside the terminals. A free shuttle runs between the terminals and the car parks.

A typical taxi fare to the centre of Nice would be €25–30, Cannes €70–5 and Monaco €75–85.

Heli Air Monaco (tel: +377-92 05 00 50; www.heliairmonaco.com) runs scheduled helicopter services between Nice airport and Monaco that take 6 minutes and are not necessarily much more expensive than a taxi (approximately €115).

The small **Aéroport Toulon-Hyères** (tel: 08 25 01 83 87; www.toulon-hyeres.aeroport.fr) is located in Hyères and served by Ryanair flights from London Stansted and Bristol.

Arrival by Rail

From the UK, Eurostar trains (tel: 08705 186 186; www.eurostar.co.uk) run from London St Pancras to Lille and Paris Gare du Nord. Services for the South depart from Paris Gare de Lyon. The high-speed TGV reaches Nice in 6 hours; some trains also stop at St-Raphael (for boats to St-Tropez), Cannes, Antibes, Monaco and Menton.

In the UK, tickets can be booked at the Rail Europe Travel Centre (1 Lower Regent Street, London SW1, tel: 08448 484 064/051) or online (www.raileurope.co.uk). For SNCF reservations and information see www.voyages-sncf.com. In the US, call 877 257 2887 or visit www.raileurope.com/us.

By motor-rail. Between May and September, the SNCF operates a direct service from Calais to Nice (tel: 08448 484 050, www.raileurope.co.uk), and all year round from Paris and Lille.

Driving

To Nice from the UK by car (via Paris or Rheims) with Eurotunnel from Folkestone or car ferry from Dover to Calais, is around 1,240km (770 miles). To bring a car into France you will need a valid driving licence, your car registration papers, insurance coverage and a set of spare bulbs. A red warning triangle and a fluorescent safety waist-coat are obligatory in case of breakdown. Drivers and all passengers (back and front) are required by law to wear seat belts. Children under 10 may not travel in the front, except in appropriate baby seats with the air bag disconnected.

Driving regulations. Drive on the right, pass on the left. In built-up areas, give priority to vehicles coming from the right unless indicated by road markings. The speed limit is 130km/h (80mph) on *autoroutes* (motorways); 110km/h (70mph) on dual carriageways; 90km/h (55mph) on other country roads; and 50km/h (30mph) in built-up areas (30km/h (20mph) in some residential districts). Speed limits are reduced in wet weather. There are speed radars installed on some roads. Note that most *autoroutes* are toll roads *(péages)*.

Roads can get very clogged up in summer especially on Saturdays and around the 14 July and 15 August public holidays. There is often less traffic at lunchtime, and on Sunday, when lorries are not allowed to travel.

Car rental. The major car-rental companies all have branches at Nice airport; most also have branches in Nice (around the train station), Cannes and Monaco. To rent a car, you must have a driving licence (held for at least one year) and a passport. The minimum age is 20–23. Third-party insurance is compulsory. Major car-hire companies include:

Avis: tel: 08 20 05 05 05; www.avis.com; Budget: tel: 08 25 00 35 64; www. budget.com; Europcar: tel: 08 25 358 358; www.europcar.com; Hertz: tel: 01 39 38 38 38; www.hertz-europe.com.

Public Transport

Bus and tram. Nice has a comprehensive network of urban bus routes and a tramway run by Ligne d'Azur (www.lignedazur.com), plus five night bus routes leaving from place Masséna (every 30 min, 9.10pm–1.10am). Single journeys have a flat rate of €1 (valid for 74 minutes and including one transfer), which can be bought on the bus; the same tickets can be used on buses and trams (but not airport express buses); a one-day pass, including airport buses, costs €4.

Regional bus services between Nice, Cannes and Menton are run by RCA (Rapides Côte d'Azur, www.rca.tm.fr). Nice's bus station *(gare routière)* is at 5 boulevard Jean Jaurès. Buses in the Var are run by Sodetrav (www.sodetrav.fr). **Train.** There are frequent TER regional trains along the coast, stopping at most towns between Cannes and Menton, with a branch line inland from Cannes to Grasse (see www.ter-sncf.com/Paca/index.asp for schedules). **Bicycle.** Nice has a municipal bike hire scheme (www.velobleu.org), with 90 stations around the city. Bikes can also be hired at Holiday Bikes (www.holiday-bikes.com), which has branches in Nice and several other towns.

Taxis

Nice's taxis are notoriously expensive; try Central Taxi Riviera (tel: 04 93 13 78 78). Allo Taxi cover Cannes (tel: 08 90 71 22 27; www.taxicannes.fr) and Monaco (tel: +377-93 15 01 01).

V

VISAS AND PASSPORTS

British visitors need only a passport to enter France, as do nationals of other EU countries and Switzerland. US citizens do not need a visa for stays of up to 90 days. Other nationalities should check with the French Embassy in their country for entry requirements.

W

WEBSITES

As well as tourist offices *(see p.105)* try the following for useful information:
www.beyond.fr – English-language for Provence and the Côte d'Azur
www.cannes.com – municipal website
www.cote.azur.fr – directory of hotels, rentals and activities
www.monte-carlo.mc – official guide to the principality
www.nice.fr – municipal website
www.nicerendezvous.com – Nice past and present
http://riviera.angloinfo.com – practical directory of English-language services, events and culture

Above from far left: the luxury way to get around the Riviera; Nice tram.

Women Travellers Women should have no problem travelling on the French Riviera, although the usual safety precautions should be taken when walking around late at night. France has one of Europe's highest proportions of women who work and it is totally acceptable for women to go alone to cafés and restaurants.

Hotels ranging from medieval castles to Belle Époque villas to conceptual modern design buildings are all part of the Riviera experience. Despite a reputation for expensive palaces with sumptuous suites and every imaginable amenity, there are also plenty of affordable places where you will still find a warm welcome, sometimes in lovely settings; just do not expect too much in the way of room service and be prepared to drag your suitcases up the stairs yourself. If you arrive without accommodation, many tourist offices have a last-minute reservation service. Book well ahead for Cannes Film Festival and the Monaco Grand Prix in late May, when hotels are full for miles around and prices can easily double or more.

Hi Hôtel

3 avenue des Fleurs; tel: 04 97 07 26 26; www.hi-hotel.net; €€€–€€€€

A cult address for design buffs, where nine different room concepts encourage you to experiment with new ways of living; try a bath in the middle

---

Price for a double room for one night in high season, including tax but not breakfast:

€€€€ over 300 euros
€€€ 180–300 euros
€€ 100–180 euros
€ below 100 euros

---

of the room, a pontoon, four-poster bath and operating table bed... There's an organic snack bar and restaurant and DJs in the bar at weekends. The rooftop sundeck has a minuscule pool and is more suitable for taking a dip than doing lengths.

Hôtel Aria

15 avenue Auber; tel: 04 93 88 30 69; www.aria-nice.fr; €€

Overlooking an attractive garden square amid the Belle Époque and Art Deco buildings of the musicians' quarter, this good-value 19th-century hotel has recently been renovated although it kept the creaky vintage panelled lift. Rooms are light and high-ceilinged and decorated in sunny Mediterranean colours.

Hôtel Beau Rivage

24 rue St-François-de-Paule; tel: 04 92 47 82 82; www.nicebeaurivage. com; €€€€

Located near the Opéra, the hotel where Matisse stayed when he first came to Nice – as well as Nietzsche and Chekhov – is now a gorgeous exercise in sophisticated minimalism and decorated in natural wood and tones of grey by architect Jean-Michel Wilmotte. Beach pebbles are an underlying theme, from the pebble-shaped pouffes and cushions in Les Galets lounge bar to the pebble lamp-stands in the 118 rooms and the pebble-floor bathrooms. It also owns the chic Beau Rivage beach, with its huge, teak-decked restaurant.

Hôtel Ellington

25 boulevard Debouchage; tel: 04 92 47 79 79; www.ellington-nice.com; €€€

This elegant town-centre hotel next to the Théâtre de l'Image et de la Photo was transformed in 2008 as a homage to jazz. Downstairs there is an atmospheric, 1950s speakeasy-style whisky bar, as well as black-and-white photos of jazz musicians in lifts and corridors. Bedrooms vary between black-and-white minimalism and a more traditional Provençal style.

Hôtel Le Grimaldi

15 rue Grimaldi; tel: 04 93 16 00 24; www.le-grimaldi.com; €€–€€€

A lovely intimate hotel in the New Town with helpful staff and comfortable good-sized rooms decorated with colourful neo-Provençal fabrics.

Hôtel Negresco

37 promenade des Anglais; tel: 04 93 16 64 00; www.hotel-negresco-nice.com; €€€€

Crowned by its pink and green cupola, the Negresco is both Nice's most celebrated hotel and one of its most eccentric, with its mix of elegance and kitsch. Original Old Master paintings and modern sculptures by Nikki de St-Phalle mix with gold-plated basins and curiously tacky souvenir shops,

and owner Jeanne Augier has personally selected the rooms' antiques and other furnishings. There are two restaurants: the haute-cuisine Chantecler and the merry-go-round themed La Rotonde. There is a private beach in front of the hotel.

Hôtel du Petit Palais

17 avenue Emile Bieckert; tel: 04 93 62 19 11; www.petitpalaisnice.com; €€

Staying in the intimate ochre-coloured villa in Cimiez that once belonged to actor-playwright Sacha Guitry gives a taste of living in residential Nice. Staff are welcoming and rooms are attractively decorated, some with small terraces or balconies giving views over the rooftops to the Baie des Anges, and there is a small paved garden courtyard. It is near to the Chagall Museum but a bit of a trek to most of the city's restaurants.

Hôtel Suisse

15 quai Raubà Capéù; tel: 04 92 17 39 00; www.hotels-ocre-azur.com; €€

Behind a period façade and built into the cliff face of Castle Hill, the attractive Hôtel Suisse has been stylishly modernised with a different colour scheme on each floor. Most rooms have sea view and balcony. The gorgeous, airy ground-floor salon and breakfast room even contains a minuscule rock cave.

Hotel Prices
Prices indicated here are for the peak summer period; prices are often much lower out of season and you may find good internet deals.

Opening Times
While most hotels in Nice and Cannes are open all year and cater to a congress and business clientele as well as the holiday trade, many hotels in smaller resorts close in winter.

Hôtel Villa Rivoli

10 rue de Rivoli; tel: 04 93 88 80 25; www.villa-rivoli.com; €

This ornate villa, built in 1890 to accommodate winter visitors to the Riviera, has been restored with lashings of charm and 24 tasteful bedrooms, plus staff who strive to make you feel at home. Downstairs, there is a lovely salon in gentle tones of grey and beige, with family portraits, comfortable sofas and bergère chairs around the fireplace, and a small garden. There is air conditioning but no lift.

Hôtel Westminster

27 promenade des Anglais; tel: 04 92 14 86 86; www.westminster-nice. com; €€€

This venerable pink stucco seafront hotel, which opened in 1880, has preserved its impressive ground-floor *salons* and the magnificent open staircase, hung with an interesting collection of historic oil paintings of old Nice. Bedrooms have gradually been redone floor by floor; some in traditional style, the most recent ones in more contemporary soft pearly blues with subtle lighting. There is a restaurant and bar.

Hôtel Windsor

11 rue Dalpozzo; tel: 04 93 88 59 35; www.hotelwindsornice.com; €€

From the outside it looks like any other 19th-century hotel, but within is a true one-off. Many of the rooms have been individually decorated by internationally renowned contemporary artists; simpler rooms have frescoes or posters. There is a Turkish bath and fitness room, an outdoor swimming pool and aviary in the lushly planted garden, and changing art installations in the hallway.

Villa La Tour

4 rue de la Tour; tel: 04 93 80 08 15; www.villa-la-tour.com; €–€€

With just 14 rooms located in a former monastery, the Villa La Tour is for romantics who want to stay in the Old Town itself. Squashy decrepit sofas in the entrance and individually decorated rooms have a boho charm. The cheapest rooms overlook a small courtyard; pay slightly more for a view over the Vieux Nice rooftops. No lift.

Villa Victoria

33 boulevard Victor Hugo; tel: 04 93 88 39 60; www.villa-victoria.com; €€

An elegant 19th-century villa with a listed façade in the heart of the New Town. Rooms are rather functional,

> Price for a double room for one night in high season, including tax but not breakfast:
>
> | | |
> |---|---|
> | €€€€ | over 300 euros |
> | €€€ | 180–300 euros |
> | €€ | 100–180 euros |
> | € | below 100 euros |

but are high-ceilinged and of a good size. Some have balconies, but the real treat here is the exotically planted garden, where you can relax in the shade of tall palms and orange trees.

Château Eza

Rue de la Pise, Èze Villlage; tel: 04 93 41 12 24; www.chateaueza.com; €€€€

Perched high over the Mediterranean, this luxurious 10-room hideaway in a medieval building in the ramparts of Èze has to be one of the most romantic hotels on the Riviera. Bedrooms have pretty *toile de jouy* print fabrics, many have exposed stone walls and stone fireplaces, and some have terraces; the suite even has an outdoor jacuzzi. There is a sleek bar and a gastronomic restaurant with spectacular views. No access to vehicles. Closed November–mid-December.

Grand Hôtel du Cap Ferrat

71 boulevard du Général de Gaulle, St-Jean-Cap-Ferrat; tel: 04 93 76 50 50; www.ghcf.fr; €€€€

Occupying the tip of Cap Ferrat, this Riviera *grande dame* was brought up to date in 2009 in a style that is opulent yet tastefully restrained. Bedrooms in the main building feature bespoke furniture, vast beds and walk-in dressing rooms, while ground-floor suites in the wavelike modern annex each have a private infinity pool. There is also a new spa, although it is hard to beat the beauty of the original outdoor infinity pool, reached by a glass-sided funicular. Americans and Russians head the guest list, some of whom stay here for months. The 300 staff will cater to every need and even the tree tops over the restaurant terrace have been manicured like a lawn.

Hôtel Brise Marine

58 avenue Jean Mermoz, St-Jean-Cap-Ferrat; tel: 04 93 76 04 36; www.hotel-brisemarine.com; €€

Expect fairly small but immaculate bedrooms in this authentic late 19th-century villa, which overlooks the Mediterranean. A steeply terraced garden, adorned with palm trees, fountains and flowerpots, leads down to the sea. No restaurant. Closed November–January.

Hôtel Welcome

3 quai Amiral Courbet, Villefranche-sur-Mer; tel: 04 93 76 27 62; www. welcomehotel.com; €€–€€€

With the best location in Villefranche, right on the quayside next to the Cocteau Chapel, it is not surprising that this historic hotel has welcomed all sorts of illustrious guests over the past 200 years. The spacious air-conditioned rooms nearly all have balconies overlooking the port, and the former restaurant has been replaced by a stylish yet relaxed wine bar. Closed mid-November–Christmas.

Above from far left: romantic view at Château Eza; breakfast at Hôtel Westminster.

Monaco

Hôtel Miramar

1 avenue Président J.-F. Kennedy, La Condamine; tel: +377-93 30 86 48; www.hotel-miramar.mc; €€

A bargain 11-room hotel above a modern brasserie with fine views across the Port Hercule to the Palais Princier on the other side. Rooms are bright and stylish with a vaguely nautical theme; some have balconies. Staff are friendly.

Hôtel de Paris

Place du Casino, Monte-Carlo; tel: +377-92 16 30 00; www.monte carloresort.com; €€€€

As much a part of Monte-Carlo's history as the Casino at the end of the square, the hotel that started it all in 1864 is still the grandest place to stay in Monaco, with chandelier-hung lobby, grand staircase and bedrooms and suites that remain firmly in the spirit of another age. It is home to the ever fashionable Bar Américain, the gourmet Louis XV restaurant and with direct access to the Thermes Marins spa and gym.

Le Méridien Beach Plaza

22 avenue Princesse Grace, Monte-Carlo; tel: +377-93 30 98 80; www. lemeridienmontecarlo.com; €€€€

Just east of Larvotto beach, the huge, modern Méridien Beach is very popular with the *nouveaux riches* from Russia and eastern Europe. It boasts contemporary artworks in the lobby and a 24-hour restaurant, landscaped outdoor pool, indoor pool and private beach. Rooms in two towers offer 180° panoramas; many of the other rooms have balconies with sea views.

Menton

Hôtel Aiglon

7 avenue de la Madone; tel: 04 93 57 55 55; www.hotelaiglon.net; €€

A 19th-century white stucco mansion converted into an atmospheric hotel with beautiful architectural details. The Belle Époque bar/salon is a delight; rooms are less elaborate, with a certain old-fashioned charm. Set in large gardens, there is an outdoor pool and a warm welcome for kids with a play area and ping pong.

Hôtel Napoléon

29 Porte de France; tel: 04 93 35 89 50; www.napoleon-menton.com; €€

This modern seafront hotel near the Val Rahmeh Botanical Gardens offers sleekly furnished rooms and suites decked out in a palette of warm colours. Bedrooms at the front have generous balconies overlooking the

Price for a double room for one night in high season, including tax but not breakfast:

€€€€	over 300 euros
€€€	180–300 euros
€€	100–180 euros
€	below 100 euros

Garavan Bay; those at the rear have mountain views. There is a bar, garden and outdoor pool and gym. The hotel also owns the Plage Napoléon across the street (guests get a reduced rate), with a beach restaurant overseen by Argentine chef Mauro Colagreco.

Vence

Hôtel Diana

79 avenue des Poilus; tel: 04 93 58 28 56; www.hotel-diana.fr; €€
This modern hotel on the edge of the Old Town has been tastefully redecorated after a change of ownership in 2007. Some of the pleasant rooms have a kitchenette and there's a large roof terrace with deckchairs, jacuzzi and exercise machines.

Mas de Vence

539 avenue Emile Hugues; tel: 04 93 58 06 16; www.azurline.com; €–€€
This modern neo-Provençal *mas* (farmhouse) located a 10-minute (uphill) walk from the town centre has a distinctly 1980s aura but is well maintained with decent-sized rooms (and efficient air-con), a restaurant serving Provençal specialities and staff who will go out of their way to help or inform. There is a good-sized swimming pool and a garden of terraced olive trees.

Antibes

Modern Hôtel

1 rue Fourmilière; tel: 04 92 90 59 05; www.modernhotel06.com; €

Beyond its Art Deco pediment, this simple budget hotel won't win any prizes for style, but it is practical and well positioned in the pedestrianised part of the Old Town. Beds are comfortable and the spotless bathrooms have all been recently redone. There is air conditioning but no lift.

Cannes

Hôtel 3.14

5 rue François Einesy; tel: 04 92 99 72 00; www.3-14hotel.com; €€€€
The most wittily over-the-top hotel in Cannes. The five floors of bedrooms are each themed after a different continent (America's style is Neo-Geo, Europe is influenced by the Moulin Rouge, etc), while Heaven is the landscaped rooftop pool and spa, and Earth, the sultry Oriental-style ground-floor salons and fashionable Mediterranean restaurant. There is also the 3.14 Beach restaurant for summer lunches.

Hôtel Cavendish

11 boulevard Carnot; tel: 04 97 06 26 00; www.cavendish-cannes.com; €€€
A characterful boutique hotel in an attractive Belle Époque building on the big boulevard that leads towards La Croisette. The comfortable period town-house style was conceived by decorator Christophe Tollemer as a homage to the English lords who once frequented the coast, with some wonderful circular rooms in the corner turret.

Hôtel Château de la Tour

10 avenue Font-de-Veyre, La Bocca;
tel: 04 93 90 52 52; www.hotel
chateaudelatour.com; €€€

Hidden on the hill above the Plage du
Midi, this is a rare place where you can
capture a taste of the aristocratic villa
lifestyle; the original wing complete with
crenellated turret was built for a countess
in the 1880s. The traditional rooms are
comfortable and the restaurant, which
is open to non-residents, moves out into
the exotically planted garden in summer,
where there is also an outdoor pool.

Le Mistral Hôtel

13 rue des Belges; tel: 04 93 39 91
46; www.mistral-hotel.com; €–€€

This is a stylish budget discovery in a
simple blue-shuttered building just a
couple of streets back from the Palais
des Festivals. The 11 rooms, named
after different winds (chinook, sirocco,
etc), are comfortably decked out in
warm colours and stripey wood; bigger
ones can accommodate three people
and have bathrooms with windows.
No lift.

Hôtel Molière

5 rue Molière; tel: 04 93 38 16 16;
www.hotel-moliere.com; €€

There is a relaxed mood at this small,
well-located contemporary design hotel,
set at the rear of a long, flowery garden
between La Croisette and rue d'Antibes. Rooms sport modern minimalist
tones, most with good-sized balconies.

Hôtel Splendid

4–6 rue Félix Faure; tel: 04 97 06 22
22; www.splendid-hotel-cannes.fr;
€€€

A sparkling white Belle Époque edifice ideally situated in the heart of the
action, near the port and almost opposite the Palais des Festivals. Rooms
have been comfortably updated while
retaining period flourishes. Breakfast
is served on a large sunny terrace.

St-Tropez

La Ferme d'Augustin

Plage de Tahiti, Ramatuelle; tel:
04 94 55 97 00; www.ferme
augustin.com; €€€€

Set in vineyards next to Tahiti Beach,
this family-run hotel in a lovely old
farmhouse is surrounded by luxuriant
gardens. The bedrooms overlook the
gardens and many have balconies and
sea views. The guests-only restaurant
uses produce from the hotel's own
kitchen garden. There's a heated swimming pool and secure parking. Most
guests are regulars, so reserve well
ahead. Closed mid-October–March.

Hôtel Les Palmiers

26 boulevard Vasserot; tel: 04 94 97
01 61; www.hotel-les-palmiers.com;
€€

Proof that good-value no-frills accommodation exists in St-Tropez, Les
Palmiers has a great location on place
des Lices, although the hotel itself is
set back in a garden with palms and

orange trees, where you can eat breakfast or have an evening drink. Rooms are simple but clean, with Provençal fabrics and modern paintings.

Kube Hotel St-Tropez

Route de St-Tropez (D98), Gassin; tel: 04 94 97 20 00; www.kube hotel.com; €€€€

This offshoot of the trendy Paris Kube has kept the trademark glass-and-steel reception cube and ice bar where you drink vodka shots in sub-zero temperatures, but combines it all with more of a resorty feel. A gorgeous pool stretches out in front of the hotel between shady lawns where you can eat in summer. There's also a smaller heated pool at the rear, outdoor cocktail bar, an indoor lounge bar and a rooftop Champagne bar where you can listen to the DJ or settle in a sofa on fake grass. Bedrooms are suave exercises in grey and white with plenty of witty touches.

La Mistralée

1 avenue du Général Leclerc; tel: 04 98 12 91 12; www.hotel-mistralee. com; €€€€

Price for a double room for one night in high season, including tax but not breakfast:

€€€€	over 300 euros
€€€	180–300 euros
€€	100–180 euros
€	below 100 euros

This white 19th-century villa near the port used to belong to Alexandre 'hairdresser to the stars' de Paris, but is now a sophisticated small hotel, with a boudoir-style conservatory lounge, an outdoor pool in the walled garden and a restaurant where the chef will personally concoct your menu. Each of the 11 rooms has a different theme, ranging from colourful 'chinoise' to manly brown and white-striped Hemingway.

Massif des Maures

Hôtel Bailli de Suffren

Avenue des Américains, Le Rayol Canadel; tel: 04 98 04 47 00; www. lebaillidesuffren.com; €€€€

Located on a secluded beach beneath the Domaine de Rayol Gardens, this curved 1960s building – all rooms have balconies or terraces and sea views – has been pleasantly refurbished in a modern, Provençal-chic style, with a heated pool, private beach, bar, gastronomic and poolside restaurants and boats for hire. Closed mid-October–mid-April.

Hôtel Restaurant Bellevue

14 place Gambetta, Bormes-les-Mimosas; tel: 04 94 71 15 15; www.bellevuebormes.com; €

This friendly village hotel/restaurant has attractively redecorated its 11 bedrooms and added air conditioning, yet kept its prices remarkably low. Some rooms give onto animated place Gambetta, but the best have a *belle vue* from its hilltop perch to the coast.

The French Riviera has restaurants to suit all styles, budgets and occasions, ranging from formal gastronomic affairs and inventive modern restaurants to trendy see-and-be-seen beach haunts and the traditional everyday bistro. Restaurants in Vieux Nice and Cannes' Le Suquet mainly serve age-old Niçois and Provençal specialities, while fish restaurants tend to be concentrated around the ports. Fusion cuisine is fashionable in St-Tropez and there are numerous Italian restaurants towards the frontier in Villefranche, Monaco and Menton. Top restaurants may need reserving weeks ahead, but it is always worth ringing at the last minute to see if there is a table. At other restaurants, try to call before going, especially at weekends and during the tourist season.

Nice

Auberge de Théo

52 avenue Cap de Croix; tel: 04 93 81 26 19; Tue–Sat L and D, Sun L; €€

This cheerful family-run Italian trattoria, with an amusing rustic decor of hayracks, farm implements and Neopolitan crib figures, is one of the rare restaurants in Cimiez. Authentic dishes include mixed antipasti, pasta with swordfish, beef tagliata and little rum babas doused in limoncello.

Keisuke Matsushima

22ter rue de France; tel: 04 93 82 26 06; www.keisukematsushima.com; Mon D, Tue–Sat L and D; €€€

Japan meets Provence with brilliant young chef Keisuke Matsushima, who trained with some of France's top chefs to become one of Nice's gastronomic success stories. Subtly lit slate tables and geometrical lines provide a suitable setting for his artistically presented creations; think green, purple and wild asparagus with lemon froth or scallops with truffles, peas and wasabi.

Luc Salsedo

14 rue Maccarrani; tel: 04 93 82 24 12; www.restaurant-salsedo.com; Feb–June and Sept–Dec Sun–Tue and Fri L and D, Thur and Sat D, July–Aug daily D; €€€

After working at Le Louis XV in Monaco *(see p.118)* and Chèvre d'Or in Èze, among other top restaurants, Ducasse alumnus Salsedo set up on his own with an adventurous contemporary menu that changes every 10 days. The setting is a rather dressed-up dining room in the New Town.

La Maison de Marie

5 rue Masséna; tel: 04 93 82 15 93; www.lamaisondemarie.com; daily L and D; €€

Set back from the frenetic scrum of pedestrianised rue Masséna, La Maison de Marie offers a bit more sophistication than the nearby brasseries and pizzerias, with candlelit tables in an attractive cobbled courtyard or in the elegant dining room. A stylish take on French and Mediterranean favourites ranges from foie gras, stuffed sardines and herb-encrusted lamb to pasta with scampi.

La Merenda
4 rue Raoul Bosio; no phone;
Mon–Fri L and D; €€

No telephone, no credit cards and the sheer difficulty of getting a table – you have to come by before to reserve one – are all part of the Merenda mystique. That and a reputation for some of the most authentic local specialities in town, prepared by chef Dominique de Stanc, who gave up a post at the grandiose Chantecler for this tiny elbow-to-elbow bistro in Vieux Nice, packing in an international set of foodies for hearty dishes like courgette flower fritters, stuffed sardines, *daube de boeuf* and *tarte au citron*.

L'Univers de Christian Plumail
54 boulevard Jean Jaurès; tel: 04 93 62 32 22; www.christian-plumail.com; Mon D, Tue–Fri L and D, Sat D; €€€

Although it looks unassuming from the exterior, L'Univers is one of Nice's very top gourmet destinations for the exquisite modern southern cuisine by

---

Christian Plumail, which changes frequently according to the catch and the market produce of the day. Choose from four value-for-money set menus or splurge on the creative à la carte.

Le Vingt sur Vin
18 bis rue Biscarra; tel: 04 93 92 93 20; www.restaurant-20survin.com; Mon–Sat L and D; €€

This friendly wine bar and wine shop off avenue Jean Médecin is very popular with young Niçois for its good choice of wines by the glass and what turns out to be accomplished, surprisingly adventurous cooking. Think twenty out of twenty for a good steak, red mullet with risotto or grilled swordfish served with tabouleh and melon juice.

Monaco
Bar Boeuf & Co
Sporting Club d'Eté, avenue Princesse Grace, Monte-Carlo; tel: 377-98 06 71 71; www.alain-ducasse.com; mid-May–mid-Sept daily D; €€€€

Although *bar* (sea bass) and *boeuf* (beef) remain the focus of Alain Ducasse's elegant concept restaurant, some other ingredients, such as chicken and sea bream, have been introduced too. The food is complemented by wonderful service from staff who maintain just the right balance between deference and informality, and there is a gorgeous sea view from the cactus-framed terrace.

Above from far left: continental breakfast; La Bastide Saint-Antoine in Grasse (see p.120).

Price guide for a three-course dinner for one, not including wine:

€€€€	over 60 euros
€€€	40–60 euros
€€	25–40 euros
€	below 25 euros

Mealtimes
Standard hours of service are around noon–2.30pm at lunch and 7.30–9.30 or 10pm at night (sometimes later in fashionable resorts). Outside these times, cafés and brasseries, which often serve food all day and late into the night, are usually a good bet.

Beef Bar

42 quai Jean-Charles Rey, Fontvieille; tel: 377-97 77 09 29; www.
beefbar.com; daily L and D; €€€

Overlooking the yacht harbour in
Fontvieille, this is a chic, modern can-
teen for carnivores that specialises in
different cuts of beef – raw and grilled
– from different breeds, imported
direct from Argentina, the Nether-
lands and the US. (There is also a
branch on cours Saleya in Nice.)

Joël Robuchon Monte-Carlo

Hôtel Metropole, 4 avenue de la
Madone, Monte-Carlo; tel: 377-93 15
15 15; www.metropole.com; €€€€

Joël Robuchon has exported his luxury
tapas formula from Paris to Monaco
with everything prepared in an open
kitchen by emissary Christophe
Cussac. Dine on a variety of beautifully
prepared, inventive mini-dishes, such
as foie gras with apricots, artichokes
with squid and chorizo, and caramelised quail, in a cossetted dining
room decorated by Jacques Garcia.

Le Louis XV

Hôtel de Paris, place du Casino,
Monte-Carlo; tel: 377-98 06 88 64;
www.alain-ducasse.com; Sept–mid-
Nov and Jan–June Thur–Mon L and
D, July–Aug also Wed D; €€€€

One of the most glamorous restaurants
in Europe, with sumptuous decor and
immaculate service. Ducasse's acclaimed
cuisine is now handled by protégé
Franck Cerrutti, taking Mediterranean
cooking to the heights of haute cuisine.

La Note Bleue

Plage Larvotto, avenue Princesse
Grace; tel: 377-93 50 05 02; www.
lanotebleue.mc; mid-May–mid-Sept
daily L and D, mid-Mar–mid–May
and mid-Sept–mid-Dec daily L; €€€

An excellent beach restaurant with
stylish decor is a relaxed place for
lunching on well-prepared modern
Mediterranean-wide dishes, including
plenty of grilled fish. On summer
weekends there are free jazz concerts
in the evening from quality ensembles.

Menton

Mirazur

30 avenue Aristide Briand; tel: 04 92
41 86 86; www.mirazur.fr; July–Aug
Tue–Fri D, Sat–Sun L and D, Sept–
June Wed–Sun L and D; €€€

With adventurous Argentine chef
Mauro Colagreco at the helm, Menton
now has one of the most exciting
restaurants on the coast. Daring com-
binations of the finest ingredients,
including fruit and vegetables from

Price guide for a three-course
dinner for one, not including
wine:

€€€€	over 60 euros
€€€	40–60 euros
€€	25–40 euros
€	below 25 euros

the kitchen garden, meet impeccable technique in specialities like low-temperature pigeons. It is all served up in a modern dining room near the Italian border, with views over the bay.

Vence

Les Bacchanales

247 avenue de Provence; tel: 04 93 24 19 19; www.lesbacchanales. com; Thur–Mon L and D; €€€

In 2008, Christophe Dufau moved from his discreet restaurant in Tourettes-sur-Loup to a 19th-century villa located on the edge of Vence towards the Matisse Chapel. Beautiful, colourful dishes combine fresh regional produce and a taste for wild herbs and edible flowers.

Antibes

Le Temps des Mets

7 rue James Close, tel: 04 92 94 07 31; daily D; €

This stylish new restaurant with very friendly service in Vieil Antibes draws a well-dressed, mainly French clientele. The speciality is generous main-course woks of sautéed beef, noodles and fresh vegetables, but you will also find other French and world flavours, such as a good risotto, foie gras, Thai salad and Toblerone mousse.

Les Vieux Murs

25 promenade Amiral de Grasse; tel: 04 93 34 06 73; www.lesvieux murs.com; mid-June–mid-Sept daily D, mid-Sept–mid-June Tue D, Wed–Sun L and D; €€€

Les Vieux Murs is a chic restaurant located in stylish vaulted rooms in the port's old ramparts, which gained a new chef Stéphane Arnal and a new Venetian-inspired decor in 2009. There is a choice of Mediterranean set menu or grander French classics à la carte.

Cannes

Félix

63 La Croisette; tel: 04 93 94 00 61; www.felix-cannes.com; July–Aug Mon–Sat D, Sept–June Mon–Sat L and D; €€€€

Drawing a well-dressed crowd in summer and famous faces during the festival, this luxury brasserie is a La Croisette institution serving fashionable fare in a sleek setting of natural wood, linen and beiges with a view of what's going on in the kitchen.

Mantel

22 rue St-Antoine; tel: 04 93 39 13 10; www.restaurantmantel.com; Sept–June Thur D, Fri–Tue L and D, July–Aug daily D; €€

This sleek dining room in a bright yellow house in the Old Town is an acclaimed address for gourmet southern cooking. Chef Noël Mantel, whose pedigree includes the Negresco and Le Louis XV, mixes tradition and modernity in dishes such as stuffed vegetables, courgette flower fritters, rabbit with thyme and polenta and fish baked in sea salt.

Le Relais des Semailles

9–11 rue St-Antoine; tel: 04 93 39 22 32; Mar–Jan Mon D, Tue–Sat L and D, Sun L; €€

White linen, beams and exposed stone walls provide a pretty setting at this upmarket bistro in Le Suquet, where the emphasis is on fine seasonal ingredients. Modern Provençal dishes might include grilled squid in frothy seafood sauce and roast veal with artichokes. There is a good, if pricey, wine list.

Le Restaurant Arménien

82 La Croisette; tel: 04 93 94 00 58; www.lerestaurantarmenien.com; summer daily D, winter Tue–Sun D; €€€

What claims to be the only authentic Armenian restaurant on the Côte d'Azur is the place to discover this cuisine that resembles the eastern Mediterranean cooking of Greece, Turkey and the Lebanon. Feast on a table full of different meze, such as stuffed vine leaves, hummous, aubergine purée and grilled kebabs.

Grasse

La Bastide Saint-Antoine

48 avenue Henri Dunant; tel: 04 93 70 94 94; www.jacques-chibois.com; daily L and D; €€€€

Grasse's gourmet treat is set in a lovely old olive grove outside the town centre, where you dine outside on the terrace in summer, and in the well-restored 18th-century *bastide* in winter. Chef Jacques Chibois puts his personal stamp on southern cuisine with dishes like foie gras with artichokes, succulent lamb with broad beans and fennel or a combination of purple and wild green asparagus; truffles and mushrooms are a speciality in winter.

St-Tropez

Brasserie des Arts

5 place des Lices; 04 94 40 27 37; www.brasseriedesarts.com; daily L and D; €€

The 'BA' offers people-watching on the terrace overlooking place des Lices, and sofas and padded walls for a more party ambience inside. The menu ranges from fashionable carpaccios, risottos and crumbles to classic steak tartare, fish with olives and herby lamb, as well as brunch on Sunday. Dress up to look as cool as the staff. Food is served until midnight in peak season; the bar opens until 2am or later.

Le Girelier

Quai Jean Jaurès; tel: 04 94 97 03 87; www.legirelier.fr; Apr–Oct Tue–Sun L and D; €€

Thanks to the efforts of designer Kristian Gavoille, this ever-fashionable harbourside fish and shellfish restaurant has gained a chic fisherman's-shack-inspired decor following a change of ownership. Fish and prawns *à la plancha* (cooked on a metal plate) are a speciality here, along with Le Girelier's own take on bouillabaisse.

Spoon at Byblos

Hôtel Byblos, avenue Maréchal Foch; tel: 04 94 56 68 20; www.byblos.com; Apr–Oct daily D; €€€€€

Alain Ducasse's world-food concept eatery, located within the ultra-fashionable Byblos hotel, has a sultry mood very popular with the glitterati. There are now two menus: Spoon Origins features the original concept that allows you to mix and match different sauces and condiments to accompany your John Dory or *boeuf tournedos*, although with a more Mediterranean flavour than the Paris original, while Spoon Now features new inventions.

Massif des Maures

La Farigoulette

Rue Victor Léon, Ramatuelle; tel: 04 94 79 20 49; Apr–June and Sept daily L and D, July–Aug daily D; €€

This simple, informal bistro has tables in an ancient stone-walled room or out on the pavement. Come for grilled meats and satisfying traditional southern favourites, such as an intense, herby *daube de boeuf*, *anchoïade* and pasta dishes.

Lou Portaou

1 rue Cubert des Poètes, Bormes-les-Mimosas; tel: 04 94 64 86 37; mid-Dec–mid-Nov Tue, Sat D, Wed–Thur and Sun–Mon L and D; €€

This restaurant has a wonderfully atmospheric setting in a fortified medieval tower which is hung with medieval-style knick-knacks. The menu here features Provençal dishes with an original touch as well as a good selection of local Côtes de Provence wines.

Restaurant Mathias Dandine

Hôtel des Roches, 1 avenue des Trois Dauphins, Le Lavandou; tel: 04 94 71 15 53; www.mathias dandine.com; daily L and D; €€€€€

After training with some of France's top chefs and then returning to the family bistro L'Escoundado in Bormes-les-Mimosa, young chef Mathias Dandine has taken over the sophisticated modern dining room in this spectacularly set cliffside hotel. The menu changes frequently depending on the local catch and seasonal produce. Dandine also runs the less formal lounge bar and summer lunchtime restaurant by the pool.

Above from far left: Restaurant Mathias Dandine's sophisticated cuisine and waterside dining area.

Price guide for a three-course dinner for one, not including wine:

€€€€€	over 60 euros
€€€	40–60 euros
€€	25–40 euros
€	below 25 euros

The Riviera's cultural programme is strongly concentrated on Nice, and to a lesser extent Monaco, while St-Tropez and Cannes lean more towards clubbing. Nightclubs will often describe themselves as '*club privé*', meaning they can pick and choose who they let in; there are also plenty of less elitist DJ bars, though.

Music and Dance Venues

Opéra de Nice

4 rue St-Francis-de-Paule, Nice; tel: 04 92 17 40 00; www.opera-nice.org

Nice's ornate opera house was entirely rebuilt in the 1880s, according to plans approved by Charles Garnier, after the old Italian theatre caught fire during the overture of *Lucia di Lammermoor* in 1881. It is used for opera, ballet and symphony concerts, with an emphasis on popular opera classics.

Palais Nikaia

163 route de Grenoble, Nice; tel: 04 92 29 31 29; www.nikaia.fr

Nice's big stadium venue can seat over 6,000 in its indoors configuration and stand up to 52,000 in its open-air version, so this is the place for farewell tours and comebacks by rock giants like Johnny Hallyday or U2, along with crowd-pulling musicals and stars of the stand-up comedy circuit.

Salle Garnier

Place du Casino, Monaco; tel: +377-98 06 28 28; www.opera.mc

Designed by Charles Garnier, Monte-Carlo's sumptuous opera house was added onto the casino building in 1879 to encourage gamblers to stay in town longer; it has a prestigious history of opera and ballet premieres, and often features big-name soloists.

Théâtre de Grasse

2 rue Maximin Isnard, Grasse; tel: 04 93 40 53 00; www.theatre degrasse.com

A striking modern venue that puts on a multidisciplinary mix of dance, theatre, circus and music from visiting companies that are usually in town for just a night or two. Closed August.

Théâtre Lino Ventura

168 boulevard de l'Ariane, Nice; tel: 04 97 00 10 70; www.tlv-nice.org

Since opening in 1992, the 700-capacity Lino Ventura has proved to be one of the most dynamic venues in Nice, showcasing a broad spectrum of current rock and pop trends from international names and local groups, along with circus and contemporary dance.

Theatres and Cinemas

Cinémathèque de Nice

Acropolis, 3 esplanade Kennedy, Nice; tel: 04 92 04 06 66; www.cinematheque-nice.com

The offshoot of the Paris Cinémathèque screens both classic and more recent movies in themed seasons and retrospectives of great actors and directors.

Théâtre Antibea

15 rue Georges Clemenceau, Antibes; tel: 04 93 34 24 30; www.theatre-antibea.com

This 120-seat theatre on the site of an old chapel puts on a varied and energetic programme ranging from Racine and other French classics to modern European drama, including occasional pieces in English.

Théâtre National de Nice

Promenade des Arts, Nice; tel: 04 93 13 90 90; www.tnn.fr

The region's most important venue for contemporary drama is renowned for premiering new plays both by visiting companies and by its own troupe directed by Daniel Benoin.

Nightclubs and Casinos

Le Bâoli

Port Canto, La Croisette, Cannes; tel: 04 93 43 03 43; www.lebaoli.com

This all-night restaurant, sushi bar and discothèque with a tented Arabian Nights and palm trees setting draws a VIP crowd and Cannes' gilded youth.

Casino Ruhl

1 promenade des Anglais, Nice; tel: 04 97 03 12 22; www.lucienbarriere.com

Where gambling combines with glitz: Baccarat chandeliers, gaming tables, 300 slot machines, plus a cabaret revue at weekends.

Le Croisette Casino Barrière

Palais des Festivals, Cannes; tel: 04 92 98 78 00; www.lucienbarriere.com

A panoply of roulette, black jack and other table games, poker and slot machines in the heart of the Palais des Festivals, with a brasserie overlooking the port.

Le Loft

13 rue du Dr Monod, Cannes; tel: 06 21 02 37 49; www.loft-cannes.com

This fixture of Cannes' nightlife golden rectangle is the best place to party in town with easy-going electro and house music in the upstairs bar club and Asian fusion food in sister restaurant Tantra down below.

Papagayo

Résidence du Port, St-Tropez; tel: 04 94 97 95 95; www.rivierabeach.fr

St-Tropez's party people have flocked to this two-level club by the port for more than 40 years. Closed mid-Nov–mid-Feb.

La Siesta

Route du Bord de Mer, Antibes; tel: 04 93 33 31 31; www.lasiesta.fr

This big, brash seafront complex on the eastern edge of Antibes spans the casino/club/restaurant spectrum including a vast open-air beach disco La Pearl in summer and a refreshingly unpretentious attitude compared to some of its snootier rivals.

Above from far left: Opéra de Nice; roulette wheel at a Riviera casino.

Casino Rules
You have to be over 18 to get into casinos and ID is required. Slot machines are generally open from the morning; table games from early evening until the early hours. For the Casino de Monte-Carlo (see p.63).

CREDITS

Insight Step by Step Nice and the French Riviera
Written by: Natasha Edwards
Series Editor: Clare Peel
Senior Commissioning Editor: Alex Knights
Text Editor: Naomi Peck
Cartography Editors: Zoë Goodwin and James Macdonald
Map Production: Phoenix Mapping
Picture Manager: Steven Lawrence
Art Editor: Ian Spick
Deputy Art Editor: Richard Cooke
Photography: All photography by Apa/Sylvaine Poitau except: Art Archive 8TC, 26; AWL Images 73T, 85T; Les Ballets de Monte Carlo 20/21T; La Bastide Saint Antoine 115T; Beef Bar 116T; Bobby H 33TR; Chris de Nice 3BC, 66/67T; Mathias Dandine (Massif des Maures) 96BR, 114T, 118T, 119T; Freakpater 35B; Michael Gwyther Jones 101T; Hemis 42T; iStockphoto 3TL, 123T; Kube Hotel 114, 115; Leonardo 96TC, 109T, 110T, 111, 112/113; Mr Mamaz 3TC, 44; Nice Tourisme 10/11T; La Note Bleue 117T; Office de Tourisme de Menton 8BR, 24T, 25T, 66B, 69C; Collin Ox 64/65T; PSD 4-2, 26BR, 66TL; Will Palmer 87T; Riastla 90/91T, 92T; Joel Robuchon of Monte Carlo 96BC; Patrice Semeria 32/33T; Silar 51T; La Theatre National de Nice/Peter Bigler 21TR; Tubantia 36T; Marc Veraat/Club 55 6-4, 90TL
Front cover: main image: 4Corners Images; bottom left: iStockphoto; bottom right: Apa/Sylvaine Poitau
Printed by: Insight Print Services (Pte) Ltd, 38 Joo Koon Road, Singapore 628990

CONTACTING THE EDITORS

We would appreciate it if readers would alert us to errors or outdated information by writing to us at insight@apaguide.co.uk or APA Publications, PO Box 7910, London SE1 1WE, UK.

© 2010 APA Publications GmbH & Co. Verlag KG (Singapore branch)
All rights reserved

First Edition 2010

www.insightguides.com

DISTRIBUTION

Worldwide
**APA Publications GmbH & Co. Verlag KG
(Singapore branch)**
38 Joo Koon Road
Singapore 628990
Tel: (65) 6865 1600
E-mail: apasin@singnet.com.sg

UK and Ireland
GeoCenter International Ltd
Meridian House, Churchill Way West
Basingstoke, Hampshire, RG21 6YR
Tel: (44) 01256 817 987
E-mail: sales@geocenter.co.uk

United States
Langenscheidt Publishers, Inc.
36–36 33rd Street, 4th Floor
Long Island City, NY 11106
Tel: (1) 718 784 0055
E-mail: orders@langenscheidt.com

Australia
Universal Publishers
1 Waterloo Road, Macquarie Park, NSW 2113
Tel: (61) 2 9857 3700
E-mail: sales@universalpublishers.com.au

New Zealand
Hema Maps New Zealand Ltd (HNZ)
Unit 2, 10 Cryers Road
East Tamaki, Auckland 2013
Tel: (64) 9 273 6459
E-mail: sales.hema@clear.net.nz

INDEX